The Poetry Of Sarah Fuller Flower Adams

Sarah Flower Adams was born on February 22, 1805 in Great Harlow in Essex.

Originally her ambition was to be an actress but poor health ensured her career would now be that of a writer.

A Unitarian by faith she is perhaps best known for her hymns which include "Nearer, my God, to Thee" and "He sendeth sun, He sendeth shower." However she also wrote for various magazines and produced a small but beautiful folio of poems and the remarkable Vivia Perpetua which we also publish here for you.

Sarah died on August 14 1848.

He Sendeth Sun He Sendeth Shower

He sendeth sun, he sendeth shower,
Alike they're needful for the flower:
And joys and tears alike are sent
To give the soul fit nourishment.
As comes to me or cloud or sun,
Father! thy will, not mine, be done!
Can loving children e'er reprove
With murmurs whom they trust and love?
Creator! I would ever be
A trusting, loving child to thee:
As comes to me or cloud or sun,
Father! thy will, not mine, be done!
Oh, ne'er will I at life repine:
Enough that thou hast made it mine.
When falls the shadow cold of death
I yet will sing, with parting breath,
As comes to me or shade or sun,
Father! thy will, not mine, be done!

Hymn

He sendeth sun, he sendeth shower,
Alike they're needful for the flower:

And joys and tears alike are sent
To give the soul fit nourishment.
As comes to me or cloud or sun,
Father! thy will, not mine, be done!
Can loving children e'er reprove
With murmurs whom they trust and love?
Creator! I would ever be
A trusting, loving child to thee:
As comes to me or cloud or sun,
Father! thy will, not mine, be done!
Oh, ne'er will I at life repine:
Enough that thou hast made it mine.
When falls the shadow cold of death
I yet will sing, with parting breath,
As comes to me or shade or sun,
Father! thy will, not mine, be done!

Love
O Love! thou makest all things even
In earth or heaven;
Finding thy way through prison-bars
Up to the stars;
Or, true to the Almighty plan,
That out of dust created man,
Thou lookest in a grave,--to see
Thine immortality!

Nearer my God to Thee
Nearer, my God, to Thee,
　Nearer to Thee!
E'en though it be a cross
　That raiseth me;
Still all my song would be,
Nearer, my God, to Thee,
　Nearer to Thee!

Though like the wanderer,
　The sun gone down,
Darkness be over me,
　My rest alone.
Yet in my dreams I'd be
Nearer, my God, to Thee,
　Nearer to Thee!

There let the way appear
　Steps unto heav'n;
All that Thou sendest me

In mercy giv'n;
Angels to beckon me
Nearer, my God, to Thee,
  Nearer to Thee!

  Bright with Thy praise,
Out of my stony griefs
  Bethel I'll raise;
So by my woes to be
Nearer, my God, to Thee,
  Nearer to Thee!

Or if on joyful wing,
  Cleaving the sky,
Sun, moon, and stars forgot,
  Upwards I fly,
Still all my song shall be,
Nearer, my God, to Thee,
  Nearer to Thee!

O Love! Thou Makest All Things Even
O Love! thou makest all things even
In earth or heaven;
Finding thy way through prison-bars
Up to the stars;
Or, true to the Almighty plan,
That out of dust created man,
Thou lookest in a grave,--to see
Thine immortality!

Part In Peace: Is Day Before Us?
Part in peace: is day before us?
Praise His Name for life and light;
Are the shadows lengthening o'er us?
Bless His care Who guards the night.

Part in peace: with deep thanksgiving,
Rendering, as we homeward tread,
Gracious service to the living,
Tranquil memory to the dead.

Part in peace: such are the praises
God our Maker loveth best;
Such the worship that upraises
Human hearts to heavenly rest.

Vivia Perpetua: In Five Acts

An account of the martyrdom of Vivia Perpetua, and those who suffered with her, is to be found in most of the histories that relate to the early Christian Church.

The main facts, in which they all concur, have been implicitly followed in this Poem. In the minor incidents, selected or imagined, and in the development of character and motive, dramatic effect has invariably been held a subordinate object.

CHARACTERS

Hilarianus, Prefect of Carthage (administering the office of Proconsul).
Vivius, a noble Roman of Carthage.
Attilius, son to Vivius.
Statius
Caecilius, a youth, ward of Statius.

Guests of Hilarianus.
Lentulus,
Naso,
Servilius
Stellio,

Camus, a Priest of Jupiter Olympus.
Barac, a Jew.
Varro,
Pudens, a Gaoler.

Christians
Saturus
Tertius
Pomponius,
Secundulus
Saturninus
Revocatus, a Slave
Testus, a Miner,

Vivia Perpetua, a daughter to Vivius.
Nola, daughter to Statius.
Felicitas, a Slave.
Tribune, Guests, Lictors, Citizens, Servants, Soldiers.

Scene — Carthage, A.D. 204.

TO MY SISTER:

Were it not so, I dared not give to thee
These pages; for I know fall well they ne'er
Can reach the need of thy mind's sovereignty,
Robed in that dress of thought all poets wear.

But thy dear love doth smile me on, past fear,
Unto thy very heart these leaves to lay,
Which richer grow the while they come thee near,
For thou dost brighten all upon thy way.
And thus, perchance, dowered with thy love and light,
They may thy nice requirement satisfy;
In thy content, I win a wreath more bright
Than Earth's wide garden ever could supply.
Ah me! I think me still how poor a strain,
And fly for refuge to thy love again!

ACT I

SCENE I.

Portico of Vivius' mansion.
A crowd of citizens in waiting. A group enters.

Voices
Make up!

First Citizen.
For what? The hour fast running out—
A crowded vestibule—all clients;—say,
What chance is there for you?

Second Citizen.
And with a wind
That comes to cut each one of us in two,
And double us all.

Third Citizen.
Ay, you may jest; 'tis none:
First dangling caps for justice in the Forum,
Then coming here to find it all bespoke.

Fourth Citizen.
Rare life Hilarianus makes of it;
Jove, what a thing it is to be a prefect!
Pay,—play,—no toil.

Third Citizen.
Oh! 'tis a way they have.

First Citizen.
And a way we have is to wake and work
On empty stomachs, while they sleep on full ones.

Fifth Citizen.
Give us good sport, say I, in the arena,

I would not mind the work. Why, 'tis a shame,
The festival at hand, and ne'er a victim,
The while the city swarms alive with Christians.

Second Citizen.
Ah! here's the man would smoke their nests for them.

First Citizen.
What, Vivius? Ay!

Fifth Citizen.
Is Rome the only place
Where they can breed proconsuls?
We are waiting
For one—why not of our own hatching?

Third Citizen.
Good:
The noble Vivius, say I, and end it!

First Citizen.
End what?—our grievances?—'tis not so sure.
A man's a man, proconsul a proconsul;
But when a man is made into proconsul,
'Tis like he'll never be the man he was.
Now, our man here—you think 'tis us he serves.

Second Citizen
And so he does.

First Citizen.
But for his proper ends:
He has a mouth for greatness, uses us
To feed its craving.

Third Citizen.
Yet he's always ready
To give us counsel.

Fourth Citizen.
Ay, and coin.

First Citizen.
And coin—
But, tell me, did you ever come at his eye?

Second Citizen.
Oh, never mind his eye—take you the others,
And think yourself well off.

Fourth Citizen.

To-day 'twill be
Nor one nor t'other.

Second Citizen.
Whoo!—he'll come sweeping through us
Like a breeze.

First Citizen.
Who is that brown man yonder?
There, close against the pillar—he's in luck,
To catch a word, if any.

Fifth Citizen.
The Jew it is:
Jostle him out of 's place.

Third Citizen.
Why are you here?
The noble Vivius hates both Jew and Christian.

Barac.
Both Jew and Christian—Christian more than Jew.

Second Citizen.
Keep close [aside]. Eh, rusty screw?—spoil is the word.

Barac.
Ay, spoil for spoil of those whose cursed craft
The glory of our nation undermin'd;
Come all the plagues of Moses hot upon them!
Think you that Titus would have plough'd our city,
But that the Nazarene had sapp'd its strength,
And craven'd with his bitter prophecy
The heart of Judah's Lion? Spoil for spoil,
While the world lasts!

Second Citizen
His tongue's as long as his reckoning.

Fifth Citizen.
At him!

Third Citizen.
Caps up! here comes the noble Vivius!

[The doors of the vestibule open. Enter Vivius, Statius, and Attilius, a crowd following. A shout.

Vivius.
Good citizens—

[Hubbub, cries of" Silence"

[Aside.]

Statius
Sometimes I give
The "good" to thee—wilt take it e'er again?
 I know the value of fair words too well
With such as these: I pray thee scant them not;
They are useful, go for much at little cost.

Vivius.
Citizens, know ye not the hour is past?
I am call'd abroad—the city's wants are great,
And like to be, the while the idle air
Usurps your place of justice in the Forum.
Hand your petitions, ye who have them writ,
And on the morrow mom, like hour shall twin
Your grievance with its cure. Now all depart.

[Citizens murmur.

What muttering is this? Quick, clear the steps!

Attilius.
The wind comes sharply through the portico,
The very sun looks shrunken in the heavens.
Poor rogues! they have been drawing in chill breath
So long, they are fain to heave it out again.

Vivius.
I will not have the breath, or hot or cold,
Of insubordination in the air
That circles round me. 'Tis the beggar's lot
To wait. What more may these be? Pass we on!

Barac.
'Twere well today that thou thyself didst wait.

Vivius.
Who speaks?

Statius.
The voice came from the right; the wind
Hath borne the matter off; the tone was strange.
Heard you the words?

Attilius.
Out, man, and show thyself!

[Barac comes forward.

Vivius.
Thy need,—if thou canst tell it in a breath.

Barac.
Thy need of me.

Vivius.
My need of thee!

Statius.
A word:
Were it not better thou didst bid again
The citizens depart?

Vivius.
Wherefore True—true—
This fellow seems no very wise example.
Within there—clear the steps! Attilius, go
Summon my people to it.

[Exit Attilius.

[The Citizens draw off slowly; a few remain in the distance.

Now this need.

Barac.
It is of silence. Need that I conceal,
(The where, the when, the who, all clearly known,)
That certain Christians meet at certain times.

Vivius.
Now you see, Statius, how Hilarianus
Sports with the city's welfare—he a praefect!
Here at a time when faction peeps about,
Muttering beneath our very porticos,
He sees a brood of those sly innovators,
Those wily Christians, build within our walls ;
Nor will unroost them, save there be some bird
Of note, whose golden plumage pays his toil.
The spirit of their creed (he looks not to it)
Would hoist yon malcontents to shoulder us,
Nay, lift the slave unto the master's level!
And thus uncheck'd they ooze their stealthy way,
Like crawling streams thorough each empty cranny,
To swell into a flood, will sweep to ruin
The old foundations of our state and worship.
Gods! and that man doth hold the power—to sleep,
Or, shame!—to drown in loathsome drunkenness
Man's eyesight out of him; while I, awake,
With sense alive, have not one step to stir.

Barac.
And know you not—

Vivius.
These Christians? Well as thou;
Long since did urge Minucius the proconsul
To advise with Rome touching their growing strength;
He dies as comes the edict; and this sloth,
That some call praefect, meanwhile takes his place;
Plebeian! without e'en the common shame
Would bid him spurn his dunghill! he will back
These followers of a baser born than he.

Statius.
Wherefore that word "conceal?" The noble Vivius
Would have thee noise thy tale, not hold thy peace.

Barac.
Wherefore? Hearken!

Vivius.
O that I had but power,
Strong as my will, to bring these vipers down,
These Christians, grovelling down into the dust,
Before the altar of almighty Jove,
Or to the sand of th' amphitheatre!

Barac.
Hear you —

Vivius.
No more! This traffic take elsewhere.
Go to that prodigal, the procurator;
He'll thank thee for thy news, though he holds not
The lawful hate I bear these subtle mischiefs;
He'll thank thee, if some one of them be rich—
Someone, who out of craven fear will bid
The ready coin leap out,—a fear begot
Upon the torture of some howling slave ;
Gladly he'll fill his coffers with thy tale,
And thou—and he—as gladly empty them.
Come not to me. Freely I give my gold
Where seems me good; but not to such as thee.

Barac.
Even to me. I would not open my lips
To have the buffet of thy breath, proud man,
Beat back my words, but that I seek from thee
A speedier and a wealthier reward.
Business goes quickly here—it lags i' the Forum :

Listen—ay, lift your head away in scorn;
'Twill bow down low enough ere time wear out.
Those vipers that you hate—those Christian vipers—
Have crawl'd over the threshold of your house;
Those creeping waters sap your mansion-walls;
Those wily birds do roost within your gardens.
Glare on; the proof I have—the proof I use;
Or give your gold even to such as I.

Statius.
What may he mean?

Vivius.
That knows he not himself:
My meaning he shall feel, and not mistake it!
Here, loiterers, citizens, lend your good hands;
Thrust out this wretch, would threat my gold from me.

Barac.
Your time will come!

Vivius.
Not that I have lost with thee.

[Exeunt Citizens, driving out Barac.
Re-enter Attilius.

Attilius.
What's the matter?

Vivius.
Matter?—a tricking Jew.
Not much—yet much, in proof there is no force
In the administration of our laws;
They might as well be rotten records all,
When slaves so beard us.

Attilius.
Ay, and such a beard!

Vivius.
The jest's ill-timed; pray you, no more of this :
Let us pass on; or choose a wholesome theme
The while the street is ridding of this rabble.

Statius.
Thy daughter be it, then.

Vivius.
You bring her name
Too near pollution.

Statius.
Nay, thou'rt difficult.

Vivius.
Go, go to her, Attilius; say I come
Soon as this audience with the merchant-men,
That takes me now abroad, has stilled their wants
How the whole city clamours for fit rule!
One moment of the calm that dwells with her
 Will smooth these chafing currents into peace.

Attilius.
A goodly hest: warmth, smiles, and sweet good morrow,
Come like a song after such winds and voices

Statius.
Make you good speed; my daughter, thither bent,
Will win the race of you.

Attilius.
Farewell!

[Exit.

Statius.
And yours,
She still companions with her widowhood?

Vivius.
And with her child.

Statius.
She is a child herself.
I mean so young she looks, though twenty-two :
She never can conceal her age from me,
I had a girl was born her very day.
So late a widow, and so fair a cheek,
Meseemeth hers was scarce a loss.

Vivius.
I chose
A man of noble blood to husband her;
As noble in obedience. Call her wise,
Who lives not with the dead. Is't not reward
For all her patience—true, she had some trial
The rosy promise of that rarest boy?
Tell me, good Statius, hast thou ever seen
A finer fellow?—one more fit to be
A treasury of the gold of future hopes?
I make him mine.

Statius.
Why slip you o'er your son?

Vivius.
Not so; 'tis he who slips from under me.
For years I tried to build my trust upon him
As soon upon the restless water yonder:
He hath no grapple for the steep ascent;
Or if he hath—at times there is a power
Looks out of him—he is most like to use it
To help another up—to pass him by;
And when he found himself outstripped i' the race,
Would stay to cool, cutting a jest meanwhile
 Upon, perchance, the straining limbs of him
Who rose above him! No, he lacks within
The earnestness to win. For Vivia, mark!
Beneath the gentleness that you call child
There is a depth nor you nor I can sound.
Thus much can I; to know there haunts the power
Shall aid the hopes stretch o'er yon heaving sea,
 E'en to the Tiber's mouth : those dazzling waves,
That the increasing sun doth now light up,
Are not more bright than they.

Statius.
Wouldst thou to Rome?

Vivius.
A Rome for me in Carthage! Let us on.
How the blood stirs for action! Come, all's clear.

Statius.
My way is to the left ; I have to wait
On Claudius the tribune.

Vivius.
Wait! the word
For Carthage. You will come again to me
At supper; there is much that I would say.

Statius.
I always gladly listen.

Vivius.
Fare thee well!

[Exit.

Statius.
Farewell!—These upward striven often find

But downward fortunes. Ever are his eyes
Turned tow'rds some dazzling greatness, till made blind,
E'en by the sun that lures, he vaguely grasps
At things beyond his reach—to find but air.
Yet with so much of substance, there's no harm
To play with him at shadows. Yon bold man,
He seem'd to know much that I did not hear,
And strange surmises floated while he spoke.
A father who has children on his hands
Behoves him take a careful heed for them.
Vivius is wealthy ; but these guesses true,
What were it, at the mercy of the Jew!

[Exit,

SCENE II.
Atrium in the house of Vivia Perpetua.

Vivia alone.

It cannot be, that I, whose heart was wont
To live upon my lips like any child's,
Should now begin a life extern, untrue,
Now that this great Reality hath come
To wake renewing life within, that gives
 A fuller impulse to my every thought
A growth so sensible that days seem years
To pass me onward. Yesterday, scarce woman,
Weak, poor, unknowing God, save in my fear
Today, a soul adoring him with love.
Yet what to do? This silence grows too great;
Hath it not even now press'd on the sense
To find a speech in phantoms? Fearful, too,
My father's face between me and my child!
The never-failing sweetest peace, that once
Would sit and watch in fellowship with me
Beside his rosy sleep, hath vanish'd all
Before that pallid shadow! Whence?—O Heaven!
 Is it thy mute reproach unto my silence?
To break it—how? To say unto my father,
I am a Christian! Oh, 'twere easier far
To speak those words unto assembled Carthage
Than one should even raise a doubt in him!
 I cannot, while he stands full in the sun,
A child for hopefulness, a man for strength,
I cannot play the tempest to his joy,
And smite him to the earth. Who comes? Forbid!
Not thou to say 'tis he.

Enter Felicitas.

Felicitas
Madam, be wary;
The daughter and the ward of Statius. Nay,
I would have staid them, but they were impatient
I dar'd not rouse suspicion ; they are here.

Enter Nola and Caecilius.

Vivia.
Stir not, Felicitas; remain by me.

Nola.
Vivia, what have I done? why barr'd the entrance,
Was ever open to me on the wish?
Why parleyd by yon slave, and bade to wait?

Caecilius.
How pale you are! Nola, I pray thee peace!

Nola.
No peace until she answers me in this.
There is a change—the very house is changed
'Tis like a prison, you lock'd up within it,
Your thoughts in you from me. It is not just
Unto die many days that we have shared
Our bosoms full of counsel with each other.

Caecilius.
More just unto those days to trust, not doubt.

Nola.
'Tis Vivia I would hear.

Vivia.
Sit thee, dear Nola—
Thou, Caecilius :—for a while wilt leave me
Questionless?

Nola.
Why press thy brow?—is't aching?
Well, to thy wish; I will not question thee;
But something one must do. Where is thy frame?
'Tis long, I dare to say, since it has seen
Those taper fingers ; though so much extoll'd,
They're sadly idle ones!—where?

Vivia.
Where?

Nola.
"Where?"—Echo!

Vivia.
There, good Felicitas, by yonder pillar.

Nola.
Ah! well do I remember that same time
This was begun, though long enough ago
To earn one's memory riddance. Here they are,
Or should be, those same flowers you fain would fix,
Because I liked them not and cast them off.
You look'd as though they had been living things,
And lifted them, and kiss'd them—how I laughed!
And something like a lecture gave to me,
That things, how mean soe'er we reckon'd them,
Had each a beauty of their own. I now
Shall lecture you, that you are idle, Vivia;
You mope too much at home—'tis time you rous'd
All Carthage wants to see you once again.
And now the festival, that trims us all
In welcome, with our gayest, loveliest looks,
Why let it pass as though it were a time
Like any other?—Watch her now, Caecilius;
What thought is't holds her thus? look! she shall tell!

Caecilius.
Oh, speak not!—how you have the heart, I wonder,
To rob her of her choice of such rare stillness.

Nola.
Strange that she hears us not, and we so near.

Caecilius.
And yet how far!

Nola.
Vivia! say, what is it?
Have all our Carthage matrons given their cares
Into your hands?—why else so fix your eyes,
And sit for hours like a thing of stone?
There's the Antigone that stands behind you,
You're like her than any living woman!

Vivia.
I would I were.

Caecilius.
Often you look like her,
She like to you, I mean,—her brow, her lip,
Could marble smile.

Vivia.
Her fine courageous breath,
 Oh, where is that? And yet to Oedipus,
Her poor, blind father—could she?—blind indeed!

Nola.
So, leave Antigone, and come to you.
What was your thought?—silent to me?—Caecilius,
You will speak truth, though it may vex e'en her;
Didst ever see a change like this?—to me!

Caecilius.
Where is true faith all change comes graciously.
When the sun shines on me I am well pleas'd;
When the cloud comes, 1 do not blame the sun,
But feel the while that there he is behind it.

Vivia.
Nola, 'tis true. New thoughts, urgent and strange,
Have so beset me round, they wilder me.
Let me but think them through, 'twill be my joy
Some day to tell them all. Art thou content?

Nola.
No, not a whit! Why should thoughts come to you,
And not to me? Plague! there's another knot;
All things go cross today. Oh, what a mesh!

Vivia.
Felicitas hath ready fingers.

Nola.
Ah!
She was your father's slave; he has given her to you?

Vivia.
O that slave!

Nola.
What slave?—who is't you mean?

Vivia.
I would not take her, save her freedom with her!

Nola.
He will not give you that; he says so oft,
Slaves should be slaves, and keep their proper place.

Vivia.
Caecilius, sing!

Nola.
Ay, do; a wanning war-song.

Vivia.
Call you a war-song warm? 'Tis deathly cold
And makes one shiver at the thought of blood.

Nola.
Vivia, how tam'd you are! Do you forget,
How once we watch'd the legions as they pass'd,
And plann'd the different garlands we would weave
To grace their conquest?

Vivia.
Years on years ago,
That ages seem, now I look back on them.

Nola.
May be; but 'tis not years ago that we
Did sit together on the shore, and you
I see you now—look'd dreamily o'er the water,
 Speaking the while of Dido;—you were fain
To invoke a god to bid her galley float
Again upon that sea, as once it did,
To bear her to your sight and to your love;
And then you said your heart was big as hers,
And could, like hers, pour out its dearest blood,
Give you a cause: and when I minded you,
That deeds like hers beseemed men, or matrons,
And not us maidens, straight you look'd away,
As you would rather have, instead of me,
The long blue line of ocean for a friend:—
And you to shrink from listening to a war-song!
But so you always were—so inconsistent!
That very time, although the sun had set
His great gold seal upon your valorous boast,
At dark I dared you cross unto the fountain,
The spouting dragon, near the steep ascent
 In your father's garden, and you would not do it.

Vivia.
Queen of my childhood! how, through all the gloom
Of ages rising up 'twixt then and now,
How pure and white she stands! as one might see
Down a long cypress-grove a marble statue.
'Twas not the letting out of Dido's life;
I ne'er did see the might of such an act,
Although my father oft hath vaunted it
In some great name, whose history might end,
"He knew not what to do with life, and died!"

Why, Nola, it was Peace—this very Peace
She would secure her people — kiss'd the steel
Ere Dido struck it home; while truest love,
That say'd its own from wrong, look'd on and smiled.
That perfect deed of death it was that seal'd
Her people's safety and her soul's dear honour.
Oh, fond and faithful blood!—might not that stream
Be chronicled in heaven for baptism?

Nola,
I have made you speak; and now to make you listen.
Caecilius, war! The Battle of the Pass!

Caecilius (sings).
The olive-boughs are sighing

Nola.
Ah, traitor!—that the song? I'll sleep; good night.

Caecilius(sings).
They bear the hero from the fight—dying;
But the foe is flying!
They lay him down beneath the shade
By the olive-branches made,
The olive-boughs are sighing.

He hears the wind among the leaves—dying;
But the foe is flying!
He hears the voice that used to be,
When he sat beneath the tree,
The olive-boughs are sighing.

Comes the mist around his brow—dying;
But the foe is flying!
Comes that form of Peace so fair,
Stretch his hands unto the air,
The olive-boughs are sighing.

Fadeth life as fadeth day—dying;
But the foe is flying!
There's an urn beneath the shade
By the olive-branches made,
The olive-boughs are sighing,

Vivia.
Are sighing yet!—O, whence that song, Caecilius?

Caecilius.
My mother taught it me; and since you came
So tenderly to raise me from her ashes,.
Looking upon me like her eyes again,

I sit and think she listens as I sing.
Sooth, but not I, 'tis music sings itself,
As easily as did the wind i' the tree
Over the dying warrior.

Vivia.
Would you be
A soldier?

Caecilius.
Would you have me? No; you sigh,
As she did ever when the song was done;
A sigh was always followed by a prayer
Unto the gods to keep me from the wars,

Nola.
Vivia, you make a coward of the boy,
And so you will of Thascius ;—as for me,
I would have fifty sons to make a front
Should grace a legion.

Vivia.
And, 'tis like, my one
May be a soldier yet. '

Nola.
Yours!

Vivia.
For a fight
Harder than any you would put him to.

Enter Attilius

Nola.
Good welcome! I enlist you on my side.

Attilius.
How! warfare here?

Nola.
Aught for a little life;
We are as dull as mourners at a feast.

Attilius.
I come for life, pot bring it. Standing chill'd
Under a portico, 'mongst muttering clients,
Is not the way to quicken up the blood.
Ah, this is well!—there is no home like this
In all our Carthage. Vivia, wert thou not
My sister, I could praise thee for a goddess.

But why so grave? You must wear brighter looks,
Our father comes to you to smooth his plumes.

Vivia.
What, then, has happen'd?

Attilius.
Nothing that should bring
Such terror in thy face. The wretched breath
Of those poor miserables fann'd him; —'tis
Blow cold, blow hot; for, oh I that prefect-hate
Burns like a fever in his veins. Would he
But take one lesson from Hilarianus,
Who loves his ease too well to have a hate
For him, or any! That he would love thee
And who would not?—my father should account
Fame to his blood.

Nola.
What! from a fat plebeian?

Attilius.
For the plebeian — Was he so? Perhaps!
I like the fat—it makes him more complete;
To see him at a feast! His eyes brimm'd o'er
With mirth—or wine, that, mounting to his head,
Look'd out again—his kindly face ashine
With all the unctuous treasure he hath stored;
The flesh of stalled beeves—their butcher (rogue!)
Did promise them they ne'er should see their deaths
For why? their eyes were buried ere they died;
Of Trojan boars, who, for their loss I' the chase,
Came stuff'd with other meats in full revenge;
'Fat fish, that toil'd with ineffectual fin;
The honey borne of bees, so heavy laden
That they broke down, and had to be unpack'd;
The oil of olive-gardens, where the sun
Did seem himself to melt, and yet the while
Did melt most dexterously each luscious drop
From the crude green into the mellow gold;
Rich fruits, so ripe upon the bending boughs,
That, scarcely touch'd, they dropp'd into the hand.
You would not have a man ungrateful? No;
He doth repay in kind the bounteous gifts;
No ingrate he! His very laugh is fat.
"Ha, ha!"—it almost smothers whom 'twould cheer.

Enter Vivius.

Vivius.
Brave picture for a butcher in the shambles!

For a proconsul—likeness of a beast!
Proconsul, said I ? no, nor like to be.
Take his name hence, nor ever bring it more
Within these walls. We do not suffer swine
To come in gardens 'mongst our flowers and fountains.
How does my girl? See how fond custom still
Doth give a license to the saucy tongue ;
We must keep compact with our dignities;
Or these impostors of the Roman name,
And offices—aye jealous of the birth
They lack—will drive a wedge into the tree,
The old patrician oak. Long shall it stand,
And stretch its arms in grand protection o'er us ;
Ages shall come to find us still enthron'd
Beneath the shadow of the might we grew.
Truce to this voice—'tis for my portico,
And not thy atrium. I have been vex'd
No more — no more — I come to thee for peace;
And all the thoughts that seek to part us, lo!
I put them off, as now I do this robe.
Greeting to thee, fair Nola; thee, Caecilius:
Vivia, why, what's amiss—the boy is well?

Vivia.
Well, and asleep; you would not have me wake him?

Vivius.
Wake him! Not I; Sleep is so good a nurse,
Right welcome is she to him. She ne'er stints,
But feedeth liberally the hidden fount
Whence leaps the torrent of our energies.
He should be strong, well nourished, and thou for him:
Today thou lookest pale, and ill adapt.
There is a playmate for him waits without,
A bold one, and a strong one!—nay, no fear
The infant Hercules, when first the god
Did stir within him, and he played a match
Against the necks of Juno's angry serpents.
'Tis finely done; the cunning chisel wrought
Like life upon the marble it hath fashioned.

Attilius.
'Tis something worth to see; wilt come and look?

[Exit Nola with Attilius.

Vivius.
Thou, too, Caecilius; for thou hast an eye,
For which thank Nature and the bounteous gods,
Hath an integrity doth guide aright
In matters of proportion; let it deal

With our fine playfellow, and bring the sum.

[Exit Caecilius.

Take Thascius to it oft, teach him to clench
His hands like it, and so to knit his brows;
'T will lesson him to strangle snakes betimes.

Vivia.
I would that thou hadst seen him yesterday;
He stood upon my knees, and grasp'd in his hands
Yon shell — his little hands!—'twas no light burden;
And when I asked for sport what he would with it,
He stretch'd his arms towards Felicitas,
Who stood where now she stands, his eager face
All radiant with the light of giving love.
Of all the myriad kisses he hath had,
Of all the claspings that have held him here,
As though he grew to me, and ne'er could part,
Never was one for joy like yesterday's :
A new-born rapture sprung into our love,
Unknown before: we were in heaven together.

Vivius.
Seek, slave, for help to bear the marble hither.

Vivia.
Wilt go, Felicitas, and see it done,
And if the boy still sleeps? And stay,—note well
The course of the sun.

[Exit Felicitas.

Vivius.
Vivia! say, why is this?
I lend thee slaves, to have them fawn'd upon,
As thou wert they, and they were empresses!
She must return.

Vivia.
Nay, nay; she doth require
More gentle treatment than your custom warrants:
Death hath bereft her of a husband's care.
You would not have me lesser than my heart;
And there are other reasons.

Vivius.
I would have
The mistress of the mansion seen in thee;
Thou wert the wife of one of noble blood;
Thou art the daughter of a noble house;

And shalt be mother to the noblest man
In Carthage! Ay, and a shall beyond. Be proud!
Thy bearing is too lax, too suppliant.
A slave should have the treatment of a slave.

Vivia.
Give me her freedom.

Vivius.
No; hers least of all.
Beneath that skin, although it tell no tales,
There's blood needs curbing. I have mark'd of late
A dangerous sturdiness within her eyes;
Though not defiance quite, 'tis near upon it.

Re-enter Felicitas.

Felicitas.
Lady, the shadow long hath left the dial,
The sun looks low aslant upon the sea.

Vivius.
So, is it? I must give the boy a kiss.

Vivia.
Is he awake?

Felicitas.
Wide-open eyes, and smiling,

Vivia.
Ah, let us go.

Vivius.
Now you look like yourself
More like. What cloud is this doth lour today?
I must have brightness—brightness, like my hopes,
My hopes in thee, the very sun of them!
Thou and the boy, who is a part of thee,
So part of them. Come, let us quickly to him.

[Exeunt.

ACT II

SCENE I.

Garden of Viva Perpetua.

Felicitas.
Yet pacing to and fro; and where so oft
I've seen her glide about, or smiling wait
To look upon some flow'r that pleas'd her fancy.
A sorry chance for rest, methinks, have they
Who hurry up and down for it. She stops ;
What looks she at?—the amphitheatre?
Has she a mind to see die festival,
And so forget? She turns, and comes this way :
I'll try and wile her from those troubling thoughts
Back to her garden.

Enter Vivia.

Vivia.
Saturus is come?

Felicitas.
Nay, madam; see, the season's coming on:
The lilies here are struggling through the mould.

Vivia.
Again another voice, and still reproach:
They give green promise that their summer's prime
Shall waft sweet proclamation on the air
Of Him who loved the lilies of the field.
Inanimate things above their natures rise,
To bear him witness ; I alone am mute
Mute to deceive.

Felicitas.
Dear lady, sure to know
A treasure safe one's own, it were enough:
For me, I like to look straight in the eyes
That think they have the rule of me,—my thought
Meanwhile, nor you nor any are my Master,
Save only One above—the Lord of all!
Come, let thy garden pleasure thee again.

Vivia.
There are too many thorns. Felicitas,
He wore them as a crown; for me, alas,
They are a wilderness! Oh, mighty Counsellor,
Would that thy human self again wert here,
To show the way!

Felicitas.
But Saturus has said,
A blessing waits on those who do believe,
Not having seen.

Vivia.
Sure they were doubly bless'd!
Who saw his face—who listen'd to his words.
O happy Mary, thou of Bethany,
Give me but one of all those precious hours
That found thee at his feet!

Felicitas.
Madam, but see
How the buds open on the olive-trees.

Vivia.
To breathe of blessings from the sacred mount.
Look round, Felicitas—all bear Him witness :
Yon fountain—was't a fountain? nay, a well
Was hallow'd by a promise, while he made
His wayside-rest in bann'd Samaria;
What says that silver whisper? Speak for Him
Who gave thee living water. The free waves
All chorus forth—We sing of Galilee;
Of Him who said unto the world's fierce storms,
As to our raging waters, Peace, be still!
The amphitheatre, e'en now it swell'd
Out of the dusk, big with this history,
That Christ did suffer death to give all life;
Me life, that have not even voice for Him,
While breathless things all utter forth his praise.
Those marble forms within, do they not grow
Intelligent with my oft-repeated vows,
And seem to live again their noble deeds
To emulate his life? I idle as stone.

Felicitas.
Dear madam, best go in—'tis chill,—and see,
The light hath faded from the temple's height.

Vivia.
The temple?—yes, to the temple! Standing there
For the last time, will I unto great Jove
Tell out my faith, and make renunciation.

Felicitas.
But think

Vivia.
And act!

[They enter within.

SCENE II.

Vivius and Statius in the house of Vivius.

Vivius.
Thus for your part in it,—how say you? Speak!

Statius.
You're a bold planner; and bethink you well
You wear the silver crown. He is the man
Who had the pow'r to send this weakness hither,
As you have call'd the prefect.

Vivius.
Had! Good word.
Though of the past, it comes with prophecy.
Look you, good Statius: what was Plautianus,
He who doth rule the ruler of the capitol?
Base born, more basely bred, an exil'd wretch,
For that low vice, the slander of his betters
What else was his sedition—his, or any?
He labour'd hard to sow his blacken'd grain
Amongst the wholesome com. Mark you, he fail'd.

Statius,
But what is Plautianus?

Vivius.
Still the seditious knave.
Although he sits at Rome, as he had twinn'd
With the emperor at a birth; grasps in his hands
The pow'rs of the state like to a petty Jove,
And they his thunderbolts; weds his brown daughter
With Bassianus, sure to strike his root
Deep in the imperial forest (note you that);
Still the seditious knave who was exiled.
His daughter weds he with Severus' son—
The daughter of this slave!—the elder son,
Though not the better. Geta yet remains,
And Geta hath the legions at his back.

Statius.
His age but just fifteen. I know it well
By this his festival.

Vivius.
When comes my pow'r,
I will create thine office registrar
Of the city's ages, save the cost the while
Of scroll or stylus. Nay, take hearty thanks.
Fifteen? The elder's very time when he

Married this minion. Geta's festival!
Had I been consul—but to Plautianus:
Ask yet another, "What?" what he shall be!
How shows the eagle of this Jupiter
The while—the Roman eagle? Eye on fire,
And feathers all astir, at each caress
Of his plebeian hand. The time will come,
Nor far remote, for the bird to slip, to mount,
And with one stoop to beak him to the heart!
Once he has fail'd—to fail but once again.

Statius.
This festival,—you said, had you been consul

Vivius.
The people's greed had been the better fed,
They should have feasted full in the arena.
They hold with you the while you find them shows:
Howe'er they think themselves aggriev'd, provide
Some tawdry folly, or some barbarous sport,
They throw up caps for you, and idly shout,
And give you godship, where before your bribe
They tongued you to the Furies. Now, dost wonder
Contempt feeds full upon such ready food?
These pleasures, as they call them, are to me
Lightnings, that clear the garden of our state
From insects, noxious, mischief-breeding Christians!
Hast seen a galley making for the harbour?
Or I mistake, she speed the coming bolt
Meantime, the business

Statius.
One moment, say
That Jew, how much had he for vouching, think ye?

Vivius.
Dog! he in thy thought? His pocket vouches
For taking all the coin that he can catch;
Say, steal—or else. He first the wealthiest tries.
 Now how to win it? No way shows but this—
That to a man unsullied in his life
Sometimes there clings a fear lest foul report
Arise to taint him; and we know how oft
Envy doth make profession of belief
In ill, where most she feels amount of good.

Statius.
He knows you not? You fear him not?

Vivius.
Fear him! Fear is the word we give the gods,

And them alone. It shames me as I think
That he could ruffle me. Come o'er again,
I should go bid him catechise my son
In his new faith, or hear my daughter pray
Unto their niggard Deity, the while
Myself did strip the household altar bare
Of our Penates. Oh, 'twas shame to waste
So good an earnestness!

Statius.
And is this all?

Vivius.
Of Plautianus? Nay.

Statius.
Of the Jew, I mean.

Vivius.
Gods! let him go.

Statius.
And I with him. My time
Already is outstaid.

Vivius.
And mine is lost.

[Aside.
[They rise.

Statius.
Wilt pass me through thy garden?

Vivius.
Willingly.

Statius.
Thy robe as well as mine.

Vivius.
No need for it;
The sky is fair. Not quite an old man yet,
For all the silver crown.
[Exeunt.

SCENE III.

A terrace. Enter Vivius and Statius from within.

Statius.
Fair skies have often clouds. Yonder is one.

Vivius.
Who heeds the clouds above, clear way below?
Ha! look you there; there is the Roman galley.
Mark, how she sways uneasy, as she knew
Despatch were writ upon the tidings in her.

Statius.
Your key fits easily.

Vivius.
So do not all into their fittest place.

Statius.
The cloud wears off; no rain will fall to-night.

Vivius.
I would there were no night—no sleep,—that we
Might keep for ever on the stir,

Statius.
Farewell.

[Exit.

Vivius.
Farewell!—key, a good turn; I thank thee.
No, he was ne'er the man to win his way.
Thus it hath always been—no, not so near
The flower of bright success within a clutch,
He turns and stoops to potter with a weed.
His "silver crown!"—I would that twenty bodies
As hale were at my beck, that I might fill them
With the brimmings of my spirit!—ay, 't would serve.
Now ends the life-long struggle I have held
To keep the just supremacy of birth.
How have I seen, in the channels of the state
(Those made to keep alive the general health)
Plebeian blood still stagnate!—I will use
The popular wave—'tis strong; for, left unguided,
Doth it not know the trick of devastation?—
To aid me as I sweep between the banks,
Back to its native marsh, this idle blackness.
I would that Statius had not been so dull:
He is the leader of your cautious flock,
The sheep o' the city,—each going after each,
The known track following,—sure, if he took the leap,
They to leap after—where? No matter, so

He were their leader. Numbers act on numbers,
Fools help to swell a crowd, like better men.
Well, we must triumph singly—more the honour:
While Vivia waits with ready crown, the Fame,
To breathe undying glory round our name.

SCENE IV.

Temple of Jupiter Olympus.
Vivia Perpetua at an altar burning before a statue of the god.

Vivia.
Lo! where, all trembling, I have knelt and pray'd;
Where vow and sacrifice, at mom and eve,
Shrouded in incense dim, have risen to appease
The wrath, great Jove, of thy once-dreaded thunder,
Up to the might of thy majestic brows,
Yet terrible with anger, thus I utter,
I am no longer worshipper of thine!
Witness the firm farewell these stedfast eyes
For ever grave upon thy marble front;
Witness these hands—their trembling is not fear
That on thine altar set for evermore
A firm renouncing seal—I am a Christian!

Where are thy lightnings?—where thine awful thunder?
Melted from out thy grasp by love and peace!
Hush'd are those timorous whisperings of fear;
Only sad Echo, roaming through the space,
Lingers upon her way, again to catch
Sounds fraught with joy, seld heard within thy temple.

The shadows blacken, and the altar-flame
Troubles them into motion. God of stone,
For the last time, farewell! and farewell ye,
The altar where my childhood's wreath was flung,
Frail as the faith that claim'd its dedication!
Yon niche, where an apart was sought, alone,
From crowds that own'd no reverence for him
They nam'd their god—is still the god they name!
Unconscious treasury of tears, that oft
Fell, like fast rain, upon those senseless stones,
That, like yon image, then a deity,
Sent no returning pity. Jove! give back
Give back those tears were shed in vain to thee;
Give back those trembling vows were made to thee;
Give back the sacrifice was paid to thee,
That I may render all to that dear God
Hath freed me from those agonies of fear

Thou reckonest for worship. Oh! to Him
Vows upward rise like springing flowers, from whom
Sweet mercy first hath dropp'd the precious seed;
And sacrifice, that ceaseth, while it maketh,
So much of love doth mingle with the deed;
And blessed pray'r, that wings the trusting soul
At once into the heaven where He dwells;
And while we hallow his Almighty name,
Doth teach us say, Our Father. Hear me now ;
Hear, thou great God of love; hear, blessed Christ!
Ye, dwelling not in temples made with hands,
Up in the eternal greatness of the heav'ns
Bear witness, all ye myriads of angels,
That, like to radiant stars, cluster in heav'n ;
Thus, on my knees,—thus—thus, before the Lord,
I solemn vow,—record it, all ye hosts,
Never again to come within this temple,
Whate'er the penalty, or death to me,
Or agony—worse death—to those I love.
Upon my head so let it come, O God!

SCENE V.

Tablinum in the house of Vivia Perpetua.
Enter Felicitas.

 Felicitas.
She's home; but what of all this care within?
Why, such another tarrying without
Of one hath liv'd so close, would raise a question;
And there are spies who use their eyes like cats,
The better in the dark. 'Tis like enough
She hath been watch'd; and sure the man I saw,
While looking out, shrink sham'd away, was one
On no good errand. Comes the fear lest she
Should peril us? 'tis like to check a pride
I had in winning her—her father's jewel.
(Christ wear her in his crown, and pardon me!)
She scarce can keep her secret; 'deed her face
Tells the whole history; let him read it, and
We all were lost; for sure he hates us Christians
Much more than he loves her. 'Twas a strange fancy
To go and tell her mind to stocks and stones!
But she is good—oh, better far than I;
And she was near a Christian in her heart
Or e'er she knew His name. She comes. How pale!
Enter Vivia Perpetua.

Vivia.

Why—why is this? these grappling human ties!
Whence that sweet aptness for thy rest, my boy?
Thou suck'st it not from me.

Felicitas.
Madam, no fear
'Tis I.

Vivia.
No fear; 'tis weariness alone:
The body is o'ertax'd, and timid made.
My pace was still the goad to wavering strength,
Lest I should miss the hour for Saturus.
Would he were here!

Felicitas.
Dear lady, as I sat
Watching for your return, a footstep came
I open'd quick, thinking 'twas his,—as quick
A stranger form slunk off beneath the arch,
Sly as a lizard.

Vivia.
In the time of shadows,
The eye, half seeing, falls a dupe to fancy;
Or shade or substance, naught is it for fear.
Go, good Felicitas, again thy watch ;
'Tis more than time, if measur'd by my need.

[Exit Felicitas.

Thy rest—thy mother will not guard it long :
But now a mist rose up 'twixt thee and me
'Twas more than tears,—as though dividing us.
Dear Christ, who bless'd those little ones, thou sure
Wilt care for him, should I— That temple chill'd me.
This is a more than weariness I feel;
A sense of death, now newly wak'd within.
Peace, peace! And dwell not peace and death together?
His aspect grim now wears an angel's face;
Though all is shadow underneath his wing,
Yet is it shelter—peace, even in death.

Enter Saturus.

Saturus.
Peace be within this house!

Vivia.
Now all is well.

Saturus.
Peace, even in death?—You thought of Him
Whose legacy was "peace", even in death;
Whose first immortal blessing on the Twelve,
When he had overcome the Conqueror,
Was, "Peace be unto you! "— you thought of Him :
Why are you silent?

Vivia.
Under thy rebuke,
Which mine own conscience sharpens to rebuke,
Not thy intent; myself and mine own sorrow
Usurp'd the place of Him thou wilt restore.

Saturus.
Lives there a sorrow that Christ cannot heal?
Nay, sorrow dies; and dying, she bequeaths
A rich endowment for a noble joy;
Dissolves in light, to bid us hold her tears
As precious dews that visit us from heav'n,
To nurture up the soul to richer growth;
Our light afflictions are but for a moment:
Is there a sorrow that Christ cannot heal?

Vivia.
Oh, question not of mine! But I of thee
Must ask for strength. Oft with a sickly child
The nurse doth wile the time with histories strange:
You are my soul's best minister; and I
Now crave the promis'd history of thy faith.
Thou wert not Christian born?

Saturus.
The dawn doth come
Before the sun ariseth to the sight.
Man's soul hath many chords ; like yonder lyre,
Which, separately struck, yield out a tone,
That is not music, but the help to it;
Or, with more aptness to my thought, say this,
The natural wind passing athwart the strings
Whispers of what the master's hand alone
Can render into fullest harmony.
So seemeth me a voice hath breath'd in man
Oracular since first he was created :
This bade the rude barbarian of the forest
To lift up longing eyes unto die sky
(The speckled intervals between die leaves)
To read the hope of better life and lands ;
This swell'd the burden of old prophecy;
Taught calm philosophy to stretch beyond
Her measur'd track to reach the prophet's strain.

The poet heard it, and did wing his way,
The more divine his song, the nearer heaven;
And in our own old faith it hath enfolded
Some types of the " to come," which now thou hast
Art, while she listen'd to the poet's lyre,
Did then create her fairest in those forms,
That thron'd on radiant clouds, high o'er our heads,
The souls of those once here, beatified
Into the deities of Greece or Rome.

Vivia.
When spoke the voice to thee?

Saturus.
First in the night
(When silence else was angel of the hour),
While poring o'er those yet illumin'd scrolls,
The urns that shrine the poet's burning thoughts,
From whence, the while we glowing contemplate,
New thought springs phoenix-like from out their ashes.
Of him I read, that glorious Titan old.
Stronger than Strength, master of strenuous Force,
Whose spirit urg'd endurance through his frame,
In mightier torrent than the blood his life :
His spirit—was't rebellion? Nay, not then
Such question did I make — the natural wind
But whisper'd in the strings — for while I read,
A pow'r above Jove's pow'r breath'd out of him.
As he his fire, he wil'd my worship down
From huge Olympus to the Caucasus ;
With old Oceanus my breast did heave;
With wandering Io did I blessing join
To give to this redeemer of our race;
And when his fate gather'd to wilder fury,
I will'd with him to sink in Tartarus,
So I might worship still, rather than rise
To reign a god, though Jove had given me place
To sit beside him on a tyrant's throne.

Vivia.
That poet's lyre did prophesy of Christ,
And yet no string did vibrate of our Father.

Saturus
Jove's thunder peal'd too loudly in the heavens,
Yet was love's whisper heard above the roar
I listen'd till it reft me of the god,
Who, throned on clouds, the lightning in his grasp,
Thunder his voice, and vengeance swift his act,
Doom'd my Prometheus! I did refuse
Him utterly. Yet where and whom to seek?

The soul asks more than fable for a worship.
To the realities of earth I turn'd:
Of earth indeed!
Then rose the gloom of doubt; for when I saw
Oppression crush down man with iron foot,
And tyranny make strong iniquity,
And no redeemer for man's misery.
Save in one poet's solitary fable,
Sad eyes, despairing of a deity,
Turn'd vaguely upward to the azure heav'n?
As empty of all governance for man.

Vivia.
There is a thought—say, would it be a sin
To track a mystery?

Saturus.
Woe for the truth,
Had every mystery remain'd untrack'd!

Vivia.
There are some mysteries, I scarce begin
To thread them, but from out them up springs love,
Flies through them like a bird along a grove,
And sings them to forgetfulness, in joy.
But one e'en now doth come to hold her mute:
Oppression yet doth crush with iron foot.
And tyranny makes strong iniquity,
Though a Redeemer hath appear'd for man,
Who bade us look to heaven for a God
Who made us, loves us, bids us love each other;
Our will is happiness for those we love,
Our power is so much weaker than our will;
But Love omnipotent?

Saturus.
I do believe,
Were love omnipotent within ourselves,
Woe were extinct. I cannot answer thee
I am but man, while He is God o'er all.
Yet as a man show manliness in this,
That I will trust the Pow'r hath given me all,
Nor meanly scant my thankfulness with doubt.
The mystery sleeps, while Faith, with arms afold
Over a trusting heart, sits smiling by
It sleeps, o'ercanopied by starry heavens,
And cradled in earth's beauty. Let it rest:
While sunshine comes to herald in the day;
While flow'rs and breezes intermingle sweets;
While birds still warble gladness out, like light
Athwart the azure heav'ns; while mountains stand

Those silent, shadowy chroniclers of time
To wake within our eyes and hearts a worship;
While yon great joy of God, the ocean, heaves
To seek the skies that mate it in his glory ;
While stately pageants throng the heav'ns by day,
 And multitudinous brightness crowds the night;
While the calm interposing twilight comes,
Tender and gracious, hand in hand with these
Her grander sisters—(see, yon unmatchable star
Now decks her dusky forehead into light!) ;
While man, the fine epitome of all,
Is master made of all, yea, more than all
Hath given to him a mind that can create
Worlds endless out of this, with leave of choice
 Of what or seemeth good or ill to him;
While love, the crowning gift that comes from heav'n,
A ray that streams direct from forth the Godhead,
 Lights up an earthborn man into an angel,
Who wings his way to heav'n upon the track ;
While for each sorrow, high and strong soe'er,
There lives a stronger good may ride the wave,
Singing the while its triumph to the skies,
Oh, can we stay to question pain — why art thou?
Nor take at once the way she points to joy !
Beware of doubt, that gloomiest, coldest cloud,
A shroud of death in life for human hearts.
That cloud doth hover near a land where souls,
Once falling, lose the will to soar again;
Where man, a godless, loveless worm, doth cling
To the earth whereon he crawls, to let proud death
Crush him with bony foot into the dust.

Vivia.
But are there really those who have no God?
All have some faith, some hope, a lingering wish,
Or a bare possible,—that is one step
Out of the nothingness that else were theirs.

Saturus.
No, there are those who rather would be nothing
Than that another should stand high above them.
He is your atheist, who would make himself
An individual god unto himself
Will brook no thought of equal with himself;
But, rather than confess a mystery,
Lest it should fix him with an ignorance,
Would coldly stand and watch the birth of worms
Out of the corpses of his wife and children,
Content with this —"You see all elements
Return unto their own."—Ask thy child's smile
Thy joy at seeing it—Is't dust? is't worm?

O man, that will not own nor God nor heav'n,
Because thou canst not spare from self a worship !

Vivia.
And Camus, he the priest of Jupiter,
Once said that Christians all were atheists ; sure
He could not think so?

Saturus.
No; but were all Christians,
What would become of priests? His vaults are fill'd
 With golden treasure yielded by his office,
His pride is swell'd by homage paid to it;
We have no priests, no flamens; all our service
Is freely render'd; neither least nor greatest
Are words amongst us ; all are ministers
Unto the good of all. The priest would crush
A power that comes to take away his pow'r
Camus or Caiaphas, it is the same.
A priest it was who first did point the way
Unto our faith by his unseemly rage.
I never yet did hear a hot abuse
But that some good had been its provocation ;
For in itself abuse is so much wrong,
It gives fair aspect to its opposite.
Thus, when I heard the Christian faith beset
With venomous thoughts, and the tongue's sharpest arrows
Levelled the while at acts that spoke to me
Like loving voices, listen'd for, for years,
I turn'd me full to meet it face to face;
And, lo! my soul was stricken with a God!
O, blessed stroke! O lyre, that sounded then
Beneath the Master's hand full harmony!
O love, that shone so bright o'er all the world,
That every man seem'd image of a God!
He dwelleth not in temples made with hands;
The temples of the living Lord are ye ;
His kingdom is within you. Thus for me,
From that time forth, did every human form
 Stand for a living shrine of Deity.
How dark soe'er, no fire upon the altar,
Still was it man—man capable of God!
Each blacken'd criminal for me became
A hope towards an angel; for I felt
The meanest slave or birth or crime doth own
Is yet a brother unto him was lift,
By promise of the Lord of life and light,
Up to a Paradise from off a Cross!
O grand redemption—true equality
Beheld in Christian love! Nor least nor greatest;
Master and slave, rich, poor, all come alike,

Blest by redeeming love, into heav'n's kingdom.

Vivia.
They who would be the greatest are the least;
They who do love the most, they are the best;
But if themselves begin to reckon thus,
While so they reckon, lo! the treasure's gone.

Saturus.
He who did love the most and was the Best,
When he rebuk'd those who would call him Lord,
Shone out a King in brightness o'er them all,
Rob'd in the majesty of loveliness,
Crown'd with this rich supremacy of love!
His burden that we bear, 'tis Christian love,
No sooner taken up than we are light;
And his the yoke whose pressure is but ease.
With love expands the scope of piety:
While pride doth hold the poor for baser clay,
Religion, weeping fond and thoughtful tears,
Gently dissolves their elements to find
Some vein of native good, by pride unseen,
That shines to prove her God a God in all.
There is no virtue where there is not love:
In those esteem'd the wise, how oft we see
A scorn and bitterness that slacks their wisdom;
They hate the evil more than love the good!
O how refulgent wisdom, love, and pow'r,
Shine forth in Him, our Saviour! Come all ye,
Or kings for greatness, potentates for wisdom,
Lay down your lesser honours at his feet.
And come, ye poets; ye whose winged thoughts
Have borne us oft to empyrean heights,
Where as ye stood, faint rays of purer light
Have shone prophetic of the coming sun ;
Ye who were once my worship, bow ye down
A brighter than Apollo now appears!
Your fabled Castaly no longer charms;
For where the Jordan's hallow'd waters flow,
Remembrance of Christ's image in their breast
Wakes up a sweeter, an immortal song,
The echo of that spirit-voice that broke
Like light upon their wave, when He the Lord
Was crown'd of heav'n as God's beloved Son.
Bow down to him, a mightier one than all,
The immortal Poet of Humanity!
Whose mind, a stylus diamonded with light,
Illumes the while it graves its radiant truths
Upon the fleshly tables of the heart
His life a poem, that will yet create
Myriads of poems, deathless souls of men,

Regenerate by his divine example!
Look at those faces that I soon shall meet
In yonder cave of death, all uninstruct
In worldly knowledge, yet His script is there.
O it doth shine for me as though the angel
That watch'd His sleep had been again on earth
To leave a light within the sepulchre!

Vivia.
Let me go with thee to this Christian service.
You look on me, and speak not. Is it doubt?

Saturus.
Not of thy truth, not of thy will to be
A servant of the Lord; — nor I nor thou
Can tell what is thy pow'r to aid thy will,
Should the fate fall that ever hangs above us.
Once stepp'd into the assembly of the faith,
Thou'rt pledged unto that Christ who died for thee,
To be the bright exemplar of his truth.
Thou'rt pledg'd to me, (whose only joy in life
Is to win souls to worship him) that thou
Bring not a weakness where we need a strength.
I have known those who promis'd fair as thou
As glories for the faith, to prove its shame;
And those of stronger seeming mould, and us'd
To the commonness of life, as thou art not;
For fortune hath caress'd thee from thy birth;
The world's opinion suns thee from without;
The fond affections glow for thee within;
The natural ills that in a humbler lot
Are custom, Art for thee hath shielded off,
Pouring the while her treasures at thy feet,
Encircling thee with all her graciousness.
And what art thou thyself, apart from this?
Timidity is native in thy form,
And gentleness that shrinks before a tone
Without like gentleness to mate with it.
I would not have thee venture on a way
Begirt with dangers, and thou knew'st them not;
Fear ne'er won courage yet from ignorance.
Think whither thou wouldst go—from what a home!

Vivia.
Under the stars, no roof 'twixt me and heav'n,
There—there is now my home! This is a prison,
Where old remembrance like a gaoler sits,
And every voice is like an iron chain,
To bind me into dumbness! And when comes
My father, restless conscience wakens up,
To never cease the while her stinging whisper,

So that I cannot look him in the face
For list'ning unto her. The world I fear not,
Its thought of me did never have a thought;
Things in themselves for their own sake I seek,
And not regard of others in them, or
I ne'er had follow'd in the Christian track.
You do not know how often I have turn'd
Unto these silent marbles, there to try
And gaze away a weariness of soul,
Forgetting in their graciousness awhile
Others' forgetfulness of what they owe
Unto their nobler natures. Never yet
Found I true dignity in any one
Who let the world's opinion cripple thought,
Sure of revenge upon the outward form,
Whose finer graces only wait on freedom.
The world's opinion! O what were it? What
The entire that wealth could give? I would give all
How joyfully!—for one approving smile
Like that which once did bless a little child.

Saturus.
Think of thy child!

Vivia.
I now could go and fold him to my heart,
Bequeath my love in one long kiss, and then
Lie down on earth, and listen for my death
Quietly as his sleep, ere I could live
To have him question of his mother's eyes,
And they did shame to look on him.

Saturus.
This shows
Like strength.

Vivia.
Say it of those poor tears,
That look'd like weakness, while they gush'd to prove
What 'tis to bear at once the dread to grieve,
And the reproach of silence. Let me go
Where I can look—can speak that which I feel.
There will be rest in this self-dedication;
So much of act to pacify the thought.

Saturus.
And for thy father? Pause ere you make answer.

Vivia.
No pause!—the answer's in the argument
My soul doth credit, as my sight the sun,

That he that loveth father more than me,
He is not worthy of me!—I would strive.
Help me! thou canst; 'tis here my weakness lies
Still nourish'd by fond custom; let me go
Where all will lift me upward into strength.
Today within the temple have I made
Calling on God, Christ, Heaven, to witness it,
A solemn vow to enter it no more!
What day so fit to seek my worship's home?

Saturus.
That home—think well!—a cavern lone and dim,
With earth above thee for thy chosen heav'n,
Surrounded by the dead,—amongst such living
As have but newly wak'd from deeper death.
If now the while I speak one shadow comes
To dim the perfect brightness of thy wish,
Take counsel of it; it may be the first
Of a dread host of fears may come upon thee.

Vivia.
What should I fear, while truth doth lead me on,
The vestal of an everlasting lamp?

Saturus.
Seek we no other guide!

Vivia.
At twilight, then?

Saturus.
Be it unto thy wish.
I will wait for thee at the cavern's mouth;
Felicitas will guide thee. Now to rest.

Vivia.
I rest e'en now—a deeper rest than sleep.
I will release Felicitas, to meet thee
At the entrance; then dismiss her to her couch.

Saturus.
Farewell! and may Christ's peace remain with thee!

Vivia.
Did not his blessing when you came to-night
Impart it to me? Let this be my surety.
Farewell!—I never say the word in fear,
As once I did.—Farewell! may Heaven's blessing,
The dearest Christ can give his own, be thine!

[Exeunt.

Night. The street before the mansion of Vivia.
Barac crouching beneath the steps of the portico,

Barac.
"Do" is their word—they shall not be gainsay'd;
Here watch I like a dog, keen on the scent;
Here will I dog his steps; out, out, 'tis time:
The dog is hungry—hungry for his food;
A double ration, blood and gold. Hark! Voices ;
And now the bolts!—they come!

[Saturus comes out, Felicitas following.

Felicitas.
Good sir, yet tell me, should we take our way
Along the shore?

Saturus.
'Twere rougher footing: so
You 'scape the watch, the city-way were best.

Felicitas.
No fear, were there a dragon in the streets;
I would my mistress were as brave as I.
Once pass the market-place, and we are safe;
The eastern cave's beyond their boundary.

Saturus.
I'll meet thee there. Farewell! and Christ be with thee!

[Exit Saturus.

Felicitas.
Amen!

Barac.
A curse!

Felicitas.
Whence came it?—like a hiss
A serpent's hiss—and close against mine ears.
Well, we have charms against all serpents now.

[Enters within.

Barac.

'Twere well if thou could'st charm me from those ears
Whither I make my way.

[Exit.

Ante-room in the house of Hilarianus. Servants bearing amphorae.
Enter Varro.

Varro.
Come, stir! How now? take you the wine for milk?
A goodly churn were you! Here, give it me;
They're calling out for more.

First Servant.
What! Hila.....

Varro.
Silence!

First Servant.
Hilari —'tis a jolly boy! our Hilari.

Varro.
Wilt hold thy tongue?

First Servant.
I can't hold anything.

Varro.
There—try the ground; hold that!
Why, he would bawl
His "jolly boy" into our master's face.

Second Servant.
Nay, for that matter, it is there already,
And of his doubling it would come no harm;
The governor would but look it back at him.

Varro.
Not if he's made to wait the wine he lacks.

[Exit. Enter Barac (who attempts to pass).

Second Servant.
Holloa! where are you going?

Barac.
With tidings to the prefect. I must see him.

Second Servant.
See him! 'tis easy said; for, seeing you,
Ay, ay, he'll do the matter handsomely;
See two of you; but each one seeming t'other,
To keep him out of knowing which is which.

Barac.
Once let me gain his ear

Second Servant.
His ear, you think,
Meantime my own may undergo a twinge.
Have you no salve to mollify the smart?

Barac.
Enough to satisfy.

Second Servant.
That's as it may be;
For here are tongues as well as ears to pay.

Barac.
There's for both pains and silence.

Second Servant.
That will do.— (To Servants.) Do ye hear?—you don't hear!

Servants.
No; we understand.

Second Servant (to Barac).
Take you that passage to the left,—a way
Where's ne'er a toe to tread upon your own;
'Twill bring you to a door that opes direct
Upon the chair of our good governor.

Barac.
The way is plain?

Second Servant.
Plain! — (Barac goes in). As that thou'rt an ass
To pay me for no worth ; thyself a kicking,
Perhaps. He knows his business, and I mine.
Now is our time;—all of us to the cellar!

First Servant. (on the ground).
Hoa! hoa!

Second Servant.
Here, bear a hand, lest double eyes
Be match'd with double tongue.

[Exeunt Servants.

SCENE II.
A banquet. Hilarianus, Camus, Lentulus, Servilius, Naso, Stellio, and others, seated. Music sounds.

Hilarianus.
Louder, there; louder! Ply them with more wine;
Their strings and pipes are dry. Jove! they shall chide
E'en while they welcome. Naso, what's your plea
For such a tardiness?

Naso.
In the ante-room
Lentulus met a love of his, and stay'd
To hold a little converse.

Hilarianus,
Ha! is she gone?
We'll have her in.

Naso.
Then no word out of him,
So deep enamour'd is he.

Hilarianus.
She is a rare one.

Lentulus.
I did but ask a moment of thy mirror.

Hilarianus.
Ha, ha! Nay, Lentulus, laugh those who win;
Thou hast a mistress ever smiles upon thee
I doubt if Naso there could say the same.

Servilius.
Our worthy governor! 'tis ever thus,
We know not which to praise,—his wine or wit.

Hilarianus.
If thou didst have as little of my wine
As of my wit, thou'dst be a soberer man
Than I am like to let thee be, Servilius.
Come, fill! and take thy fill, and praise thy fill
For never did the god for me—bright Bacchus

(Camus, with reverence to almighty Jove),
Borrow his beams of Sol for better deed;
Ha! sine cerâ—look you, that's the thing.

Lentulus.
I have some drinking-vessels newly come
From Italy; they are of rare device.
One hath a dancing faun for pedestal;
The eyes, the face, the limbs, are so on the move,
You wonder how the cup escapes the trick.

Hilarianus.
Ha! that's a fair conceit r I like the hint,
To take good wine from out bad custody.

Lentulus.
Another thus, borne on th' uprais'd arm
Of a bewitching Venus, who, in sport,
Would lift the cup beyond the reach of Cupid.
With cunning grace she turns in search for him;
While he, as sportive, flies up to the brim,
And there doth lip the draught with up-turn'd wing
Not the first time Cupid hath serv'd as handle
For a flowing bowl.

Servilius.
Capital!

Lentulus.
A third is—

Hilarianus,
Nay, Lentulus, thine own doth stand untouch'd.
(Aside.) This choking prose of hes and shes!—Sing,
Stellio!

Stellio.
Give me a moment.—(To Naso) There is no song in me.
Yon silent, sourest-visag'd priest—'tis he
Who pinches all the music out of us.

A Guest.
Oh, fear not him; look at the wine he takes!

Naso,
Nay, so much wine coupled with so much silence
Says, beware!

Stellio,
Why hath the prefect such a guest?

Naso.
For skeleton unto the feast, perchance.

Stellio.
Where is the veil?

Naso.
Hilarianus knows,
Once have a priest for enemy, good bye
To peace! Brave feasts, and he unbidden!
You were a wit to find a better scheme
To kindle up his wrath.

Stellio.
Why shame such bounties?
Such a starvation-face is a rebuke.

Naso.
Is that your quarrel? Why, you take away
All credit from the only thing where he
Doth fail in semblance to fulfil in deed.
For me, I like to see him where he sits
Beside our bright-faced praefect; 'tis to look
At once upon the full moon and the edge.

Hilarianus.
Now, Stellio, your moment's gone ; dash into it.

Stellio (sings).
Cymbals for me!

Hilarianus.
Ha, ha] that is the song. Cymbals, strike up!

[Flourish of cymbals.

STELLIO (sings)
Cymbals for me
Flash'd high in air,
By curving arms
Over streaming hair:
'Twas thus she led the way along,
Who weaves the garland of my song.

Sun-kiss'd brows with vine-wreaths crown'd,
Dropping purple dews around;
Eyes whose glances, bee-like, wing
Honey sweetness with a sting!
Ripe lips, rose-fed, ever bright'ning,
Love doth quiver round like lightning;
Limbs with curving grace so rife,

Their drapery rises into life;
Feet like air; the dizzy head
 Loses the earth whereon they tread.
'Twas thus she led the way along,
Who weaves the garland of my song.

Chorus.
Cymbals for me
Flash'd high in air,
By curving arms,
Over streaming hair:
'Twas thus she led the way along,
Who weaves the garland of my song,

[Another flourish.

Hilarianus,
Ha! ha! 'tis bravely sung. Here, keep this cup.

Enter Varro.

Varro.
My lord, a messenger from Rome

Hilarianus.
Tell him
Freely to sleep after his journey. Go!
Where was I? Ha! the cup; —'tis thine, good Stellio.
No beauty—not like those of Lentulus ;
For it belongs to one who never cares
What the cup be, so that good wine doth fill it,
'Tis gold, and when full brimm'd, the feast half over,
No light one, on my conscience. Quick, another.
And now, to give thy song its worthiest crown,
Rise all of ye, I pour libation out
Unto our queen of Carthage. So she was
And is, though one doth ne'er get sight of her ;
Vivia Perpetua — the queen of Carthage!

[Barac appears.

Why, what black rogue are you? Here, knaves, a bowl;
Drink, and give 'count with brighter face. Thy beard
Shall be the torch else.

Barac.
Kindle other fires,
Shall warm you double-wise.

Camus.
I know the man;

Let him speak on.

Barac.
Better confer apart.

Hilarianus.
And best, that you
Sluice back your speech into your throat, and then
Sneak quietly out. How you came in, the gods
Do know; not I.

Camus.
Dismiss him not.
Take thou my counsel, prefect; listen to him;
The omnipotent Jove doth often time decree
The voice of Fate to speak for years in moments,
E'en by an oracle so mean as this.

Hilarianus.
Good friends, scarce gone ere I am back again ;
Make it a merrier time amongst ye all,
And I'll forgive ye, though ye say my loss
Was so much gain.

Stellio.
See you, the priest hath done it!

[Camus, Hilarianus, and Barac, come forward.

Camus.
Speak freely.

Hilarianus.
How or what, so it be brief,

Barac.
I bring you certain knowledge, and will guide
To where they meet, within a burial-cave
At twilight, Christians who....

Hilarianus.
Oh, the old story !
Enough; there lies your way.—Come, Camus.

Barac.
Yet,
There's wealth for you to seize—pow'r to be crush'd.

Camus.
A steady witness stands within his eye.

Hearken, lord governor! Our sacred coffers,
Wherewith we serve the gods, are poorly grac'd :
You have demands upon you that 'twere wise
To have well answer'd.

Hilarianus.
Ay, but all the rich
I know, long since are pluck'd; and they, the poor
Who help'd us pluck them, rotted; save perhaps
A bone or two clean pick'd by hungry vultures.
Such work I always hate. The emperor
Should pay us better, and prevent the need.
Take hence thy chamel-stories. Twilight, man!
And in a burial-cave, March in its nones!
If this the worship that their God exacts,
The service sure of such a deity
Is hard enough without being punish'd for it.
My marrow shivers at the naked thought!
What, Camus! fear their making converts, eh?
Leave we this cloud, and back into yon sunshine.

Camus.
Not yet.

Hilarianus.
Some wine here, Stellio—anybody.

Barac.
What wouldst thou say—and, mark me! I have proof—
If I should tell thee that thy queen of Carthage,
Whose name but now was ringing in thy roof,
Was one among them?

Hilarianus.
Oh, the man is mad! [Drinks.

Camus.
No more than thou, nay, less; let thine eye see
The gold beneath that wine.—Speak on!—thy proof?

Barac.
Long since I chanc'd to know (how, matters not)
That certain slaves within the house of Vivius
 Had by a busy meddler 'mongst these Christians
One Saturus by name—been made his converts;
One of these slaves hath sometime been preferr'd
Unto Perpetua's household; and of late
This convert-making man hath found his way
Over her threshold. I have seen him cross it;
Have watch'd them walk together in her gardens,
Screen'd by a fountain close upon their path;

Have heard the cursed name upon their lips
Of him who help'd to strip us of our glory;
(I am a Jew, so you may trust my hate)—
Of him whose name, unless you check its pow'r,
Will do the like for you and all your gods.

Camus.
(Aside) There could not come a fitter time for this:
The festival of Geta close at hand;
The father, he is wealthy; and, besides,
Hath too much sway over the citizens
Too little of submission unto us.
The daughter weak, weak as all women are,
And beautiful, as would all women were!
Come, procurator, sir, Hilarianus,
You must bestir in this, and promptly too ;
The emperor's edict hath too long repos'd;
The people's pleasures are concern'd herein;
Examples must be made — the gods require it!

Hilarianus.
I see it all! The rheumatism, too,
That cursed seat of justice always gives me
The hours I've lost with their infernal squabbles!
And for your doings in the amphitheatre,
Confound them all! Give me a quiet life;
Or if you must have savage beasts for sport,
Sleek them to fit our Bacchanalia; then
Harness them safe unto a car, shall draw
Our jolly god through crowds all ivy-crown'd,
With Pan to lead them on to sound of reeds,
Cymbals and flutes, and all the instruments.
And you shall be Silenus ; and we'll have
My queen of Carthage there for Semele;
And I'll be Jupiter — by Jupiter!
Ha! ha! You frown. Ah, you're a cunning priest;
Methinks (with reverence to almighty Jove),
You were not loath to play his part in it!
What said I ? I'm profane ; the gods forgive us!

Camus.
That signet—so—now back unto the guests
Are gaping, greedy for thee, at thy back.
Follow me, Jew; you have the instant proof.

Barac.
Sure;—but my reward?

Camus.
By all my gods, equal to thy desert!

[Exeunt Camus and Barac; Hilarianus reels back to the table; a shout; scene closes.

SCENE III.

A guard-house. Soldiers gaming; a gladiator and others looking on.

First Soldier.
Good luck, good rattle-bones! and for a wish,
I'll back my wager;—here's your victory !

Second Soldier.
Who is your match?

Gladiator.
I neither know nor care.

Second Soldier.
What! sulky?—eh!

First Soldier.
Hurra! Venus again!
Smile up !—we win the day.

Gladiator.
Where is the use?
Three times I've play'd for life, for life or death,
And won my game; but he who fights with me,
 Although he has it, up go all their thumbs;
And up stands he alive, and walks away.
They call this sport — I call it make-believe;
Tames us to fight like children 'stead of men,
Filling our school with craven, beaten slaves.
Give me the good old ways. If I were down,
I'd have my death, my due ; no thumbing me,
Except the backward way.

First Soldier.
Well done, my boy
My wager 'gainst the world. Were all like you,
Then should we have a festival were worth.

Second Soldier.
Not till we-have a prefect wide awake.

Third Soldier
Order there!—order! We are of the state,
And must support its dignity.

Second Soldier.

Ay, true;
It needs a heavy prop.

Enter a Lictor, with Barac.

Lictor.
Up, soldiers!—ho!
To your feet. Ready, and out! Here's news to stir ye
 Service that's sport, and better sport beyond.

First Soldier.
Who is your slinker?

Lictor.
Learn the trick of him;
And slink like moles, with eyes as keen as lynxes,
Towards the cave east of the aqueduct.
First to the market-place to hear the edict,
And then to seize them at their sport — a covey
Of Christians!

Soldiers.
Ha! huzza!

Barac.
No time to lose ;
The trap hath open doors; they may escape.

First Soldier,
Put up your tongue; we'll pounce upon them sweetly:
Look you, that is the spring.

Barac.
Hold! hold!

Second Soldier.
No tiger
In the arena

Lictor.
See you harm them not;
Bring them alive!

First Soldier.
I would not rob die beasts
By rubbing off their bloom.

Second Soldier.
Was e'er such luck?
Ha, sulky!—they'll divide the sport with you.

Gladiator.
Beware they try it not on you. I saw
A Christian once strangle in the arena
A savage wolf. Lean, lithe, and swift as sure,
The creature sprang at him with hungry howl;
His eye a ruddy fire, his crimson laps
Drawn tightly up above a show of teeth
That glitter'd joyful at their coming meal.
The man stood still to wait him (as the death),
Nor made or sign or move; when in a twink
His hands had grasp'd the wolf about the throat
The next, he dropp'd him dead into the sand
Lightly, as one might throw away a weed;
And yet they slew that man, and spare our cowards!

Lictor.
Come, all is ready.

First Soldier (to Barac).
Lead you on, old mole!
Don't draw too far ahead into the dark.

Lictor.
Steady ; and follow up.

[Exeunt.

SCENE IV.
Seashore; early twilight; mouth of a burial-cave. Vivia and Felicitas watching.

Felicitas.
This tarrying, with the strangeness of the place,
Dear lady, sorteth not with one like thee.

Vivia.
There is a spirit haunts about the cave
That holds me rooted, as I were a plant
Had found a rest beneath the rocky arch.
No strangeness is there, save that it is strange
I should feel none.

Felicitas.
Think you that Saturus
Would choose the seaward way?—some new-fall'n rock
Hath thwarted him, and sent him through the city.

Vivia.
How still and black it lies!—death without hope!
While yonder red, unsteady pharos-light

Gleams like an earthborn and earth-dying joy,
Fitfully wavering with each passing breath :
The sea beneath, its restless chronicler,
Time's mighty clepsydra, that marks his pace
By wave on wave emptied upon the shore.
Brief joys, light flames, that scarce do bum ere die ;
Blackness of death, and restlessness of time,
If that were all.—
The heav'ns! Up to the heav'ns for hope, for light.
Yon crescent moon, and those intelligent stars,
Sure they are in communion. Are they rapt
In the eternity they promise?—these Ling'ring
(while all those countless multitudes
Have left the sky unto the coming dawn),
Lost in their converse deep. Ye beautiful!
That draw up what was pain from out the heart,
And fill the empty void with heavenly peace.
For ever there! Ye are the very same
That o'er the lowly home in Nazareth
Have nearer come, to light the silent vigil
Of Him who slept not, while he sought the way
To bring our souls to everlasting rest.

Felicitas.
Lady, it is an awful thing to think
That all yon sleeping city should be heathen.

Vivia.
And yet the stars of heav'n shine over all.
What are ye, that ye clasp us to your light?
Too far for knowledge, yet how near for love!
Ye sing to us. A harmony divine
Goes on the while I look, as though I listen'd,
As though ye heard and answer'd to the choir
Of seraphs praising round the throne of God
Glory to God alike their song and yours:
O earth, hast thou no echo for such strain?
What comes? Voices there are — no! not I' the air;
It sings beneath my feet.

Felicitas.
Lady, thy fancy sings.

Vivia.
Nay, bend thine ear, and listen.

Felicitas.
True; 'tis they
Within the cave : sure Saturus is there.

Vivia.

Hush!—'tis his footstep—fleet, yet even-pac'd;
I know it well.

Enter Saturus.

Saturus.
Here!—ye have waited long?

Vivia.
'Twere meet we wait for thee, not thou for us.

Saturus.
Pause ere ye enter; for within this hour
I have both heard and seen that peril waits.
If thou didst know the passage to yon cave,
That leads to life in Christ, were pav'd with death,
Wouldst enter it?

Vivia.
I would.

Felicitas.
What hath befall'n?

Saturus.
Quickly within, and there thou shalt know all.
The rock is hewn into descending steps ;
They are rough — plant firm your foot; there's light beyond.

[They enter the cave.

SCENE V.

A cave of sepulchre dimly lighted.
Tertius, Pomponius, Saturninus, Secundulus, Testus, and others.

(They sing.)
Oye fearful shepherds,
Watchers in the night,
When the heav'ns open'd.
Darkness into light;
Little knew ye who was he,
The Saviour of the world to be,
Lord of men and angels; when
Rang their song throughout the sky
Glory be to God on high;
Peace on earth, good-will to men!

Enter Saturus, Vivia, and Felicitas.

O we happy Christians,
Watchers in the night,
Joyful to our darkness
Comes the heavenly light;
For we know the Lord is he,
The Saviour of the world to be.
Let us with the angels, then,
Sing that song yet in the sky
Glory be to God on high;
Peace on earth, good-will to men!

Tertius.
What voice ariseth like a flame amongst us?

Saturus.
A fiery voice is calling from without,
The voice of danger.

Secundulus.
Lo! our teacher comes.

Saturus.
To bring a twofold gift—knowledge of peril,
And new example how to meet it bravely.
Say I aright?

Vivia.
I will not fail.

Revocatus.
Know you?

Felicitas.
Listen.

Saturus.
My Christian brothers! Say we had a friend,
A friend ne'er seen, but whose surpassing love
So cleav'd to us, that he did live for us,
Did die for us, left legacy with us,—
A promise rich, of an enduring home
In a far, happy country; where the days
No more shall darken with the coming shadow
Of a toil-burden'd morrow; and our woes
Shall lay them down to never-waking sleep;
Where for this cavern dim, Death's treasury
Who revels, grinning like a miser gaunt
Over his gotten dust,—we shall behold
Him, that dear friend, who gives at once to us
Life, light, and glorious immortality!

Would not the fate be welcome, whatsoe'er
Would bear us to such home, to such a friend?

Tertius.
My son, be plain; these are but simple men.

Saturus.
It was to simple men our Master spoke
In parables; I would but waken love
Love, that disarmeth danger of his sting.

Saturninus.
The enemy are upon us! Let them come!
I would it were Christ's will that we might fight,
As those of old, the battles of the Lord
With sword and sinew.

Tertius.
Peace! my son.

Pomponius.
The edict!
They have proclaim'd

Saturus.
They have; e'en now I heard it
Read o'er a gleaming watch-fire in the Forum;
Mutter'd! the words came hurriedly and low,
Scarce taking aim beyond the speaker's ear.
Soldiers, with glittering eyes and ready arms,
Savage and grim, show'd in the lurid light
As ready for their prey;—the place, the time,
This dragging of the law from out its sleep,
Betokens instant act.

Tertius.
Let us disperse!
Some take the eastern way, and some the west.

Saturus.
Tarry!—nor fly ye like to timid sheep ;
But meet the hour like men. Behold, my brothers,
Vivia Perpetua! Lo! that fragile form
Roots firmly to the earth, as it would raise
An immortality from out dead dust!
E'en from the paleness of resolved brows,
Ye timorous, gather strength, and bid your own
Now fix with purpose of a settled soul.

Voices
What should we do?

Saturus.
For Christ? Oh, what for him,
Who waits for us in heaven? To hear his voice
Say, "Come to me, ye blessed of my Father;
Well done, ye faithful servants of the Lord!"
What will ye do for Christ? Oh, what for him,
Ye whom he chose for his elect; ye poor,
Whose daily bread is earn'd by daily toil
(For ye he did elect to dwell amongst;
Ye poor, how rich by this election made!):
Not in high places, where the great resort,
(Save to proclaim, that of one blood are made
All nations and all families of earth),
Did he frequent, but with the lowly-born,
Himself the lowliest,—the manger-cradled!
What will ye do for Christ, ye wanderers?
He liv'd for you a wayside wanderer,
Who had not where to lay his head;—no rest,
Save when he drew apart, away from all,
In the Judaean mountains, there to seek
His spirit's peace in solitude with God,
Thence to return (like the descending stream
That went along with him) to carry joy
Into the thirsty valleys! What for him,
Ye slaves, redeem'd to freedom evermore;
A freedom charter'd in his book of life,
Sealed with his precious blood? Oh, what for him,
Who, though apart in mighty isolation
Of his most high supremacy with God,
Did yet draw nearer to us in his love
Than e'en the mothers who did give us birth.
Oh, answer! put your hearts into your speech,
And warrant both by act. Oh, what for him,
Our sovereign Lord, our Counsellor, our Friend!

Saturninus.
Or fight or die for him!

Secundulus.
Or lay down life without one sigh for him,
As willingly as though it were his sleep,
Who, freed from toil or taunt, did lay him down
Under the willows, where the wind-swept harps
Still echoed true the praises of his God
By Babylon's sad waters. Rest—in him!

Tertius.
"A crown of glory is the hoary head!
So spoke the Psalmist. At the foot of Christ
I lay this earthly crown, praying of him

To grant a heavenly, even though the cost
Be martyrdom.

Pomponius.
And I these lustier limbs
And longer term of days. We die but once,
But through his grace we live for evermore.

Felicitas.
I would I had a better life to offer;
Mine is too poor to give
To him who came to save
The stricken slave;
To bid us rise
From death in dust like this, to meet him in the skies!

Christ, I will live for thee,
As thou for me!
Christ, I will die
Bleeding for thee, as thou for me on Calvary!

Revocatus and Felicitas
Christ, I will live for thee,
As thou for me!
Christ, I will die
Bleeding for thee, as thou for us on Calvary!

Saturus
And Testus hath no voice?—he hath a life.

Testus.
I'm loath, sir, now to part with it; I scarce
Do want a better: all goes different.
There's no more darkness now within the mine;
I seem to take the daylight down with me;
The pickaxe and the spade ply all so light,
They clink a pleasant tune; and I the while
Sing by the side of them the hymn that says,
There is a Lord above us, who doth love
 E'en the poor miner well as other men.
Christ loves the poor;
Unto his door He bids us knock and enter, ne'er denies us.
He asks no payment
For food or raiment;
But without price or money, all he buys us.
He knows our want,
He ne'er doth scant;
The oftener we beg, the more he giveth.
The more we crave,
The more we have;
And what from him we have, it ever thriveth.

Oh, poor estate,
By love so great
Made rich in goods beyond all earthly glory!
Where'er I go,
Above, below,
Still shall the Lord of love be all my story.

Saturus.
Keep to that tune when they would question thee.

Testus.
I'm poor of speech; there's nothing more to say.

Saturus.
Now let us part;—perchance no more to meet
Till we are one in heaven with our Father.
Let us not hymnless go for the first time,
When we may mingle voices for the last!
Oh, give me this reward for all the care
Hath watch'd your growing souls,—for all die love
That still can only reckon it as joy;
With unperturbed hearts, with souls resolv'd,
With voices steadied by a holy trust,
Once more the hymn that we so oft have sung,
As now—when light was gaining on the darkness.
Brothers, once more! then all depart in peace.

[They all sing.

Part in peace! Christ's life was peace,
Let us breathe our breath in him!
Part in peace! Christ's death was peace,
Let us die our death in him!
Part in peace! Christ promise gave
Of a life beyond the grave,
Where all mortal partings cease.
Part in peace!

[They separate.

(Echo.) "Peace!"

ACT THE FOURTH.

SCENE I.

In the house of Hilarianus.

Hilarianus.

To rise so scant of rest, with ugly dreams
That halve with truth in waking! I was weak
To let the signet go. Say, wine is strong,
And I submiss to an all-potent master;
Nay, call him weak who sharpens up the ears
But to devour a mouldy tale, to him
How profitless, how troublesome to me!
Now will the trash o' the suburbs come in swarms,
All buzzing of these twilight owls — thus wise,
They strive to keep their hooting to themselves.
Who's the intruder? Keep all out, I say !
How, Camus, what's amiss? Last night, what was't?
 Something I said,—beshrew this tongue of mine,
Beshrew my memory, sulking at its back.
Pardon me, gods, whatever!

Enter Camus.

Camus.
Up betimes!

Hilarianus.
No sleep for dreaming of my signet's loss;
All's safe, I see.

Camus.
Not so; the work not done.
We have secur'd some baser of the brood;
But in dividing, as they left their haunt,
The wealthier have 'scaped us.

Hilarianus.
Said I not?
Ne'er frown; I know not what—already gone.
My recollection barely serves with this,
A hairy face, a pair of greedy eyes;
I e'en forgot my signet was allow'd
To hands of trust.

Camus.
Or you or it must serve
To arrest Perpetua.

Hilarianus.
How! on that sordid babble
Go with an armed force, and, all unwam'd,
Drag forth a noble lady from her home?
The praefect dares not do it, and the man
Stands up against such outrage!

Camus.

Scrupulous?
You have good reasons, doubtless. Will you see
The messenger from Rome? He waits without.

Hilarianus.
Ay, good; ho, Varro!—good; 'twill change the theme.

Enter Varro.

That Roman budget!

Varro.
Ay, my lord.

[Exit.

Camus.
You dream'd
The signet lost, you say? Almighty Jove!

Enter Messenger.

Hilarianus.
Your news!

Messenger.
'Tis here.

Hilarianus.
Enough of it to serve
For twenty changes upon twenty themes!
Wait not, but quick convert your wants to pleasures.

Camus.
What moves you?

[Exit Messenger.

Hilarianus.
Look you here; some meddling pest
Hath stirr'd the emperor' bout these wretched Christians.

Camus.
Lo! how the gods attest their minister.
Lo! how their voices visit us in dreams.
How clearly seen the hand of Jove in this,
Pointing your duty ere it be too late;
Ere, for your slackness in their sacred cause,
The emperor doth depose you from your rule!

Hilarianus.

Depose!

Camus.
By timely zeal you may escape.
The gods this signet trust with me, to hold
As surety for thine office,—by fit use
To steady up this slipping confidence.

Hilarianus.
What should I do? My thoughts can't open their eyes;
My wits are all a-yawn for want of sleep.

Camus.
Go, settle them, and dream your signet safe.
The scroll—

Hilarianus
There's more to read;—what is it?—see;
There! I commit the whole into your hands.

[Exit Hilarianus.

Camus.
What, ho! the lictors!

SCENE II.

Vivius seated. Citizens in waiting.

Vivius.
The next?

Third Citizen.
The turn is mine.

Second Citizen.
I say, 'tis mine.

Vivius.
You come to settle quarrels, not to breed them.
Speak you, the elder — you have fewer days.

Second Citizen.
Our quarrel's made; his telling first his story
Will give it him his way.

Vivius.
 I bade you speak.

Third Citizen.
Please you, I have an orchard stands hard by
His dwelling; 'twixt us stood a swerving wall
That left three goodly trees upon my lot,
Three of the goodliest there. 'Tis said the wind
(A keen one) shook the wall about die curve;
And straight this man builds up again in line,
And takes these trees, my right, away from me.

Vivius.
How answer you?

Second Citizen.
That I'm a mason, sir;
My character's concern'd. Would you employ
A mason who did build a crooked wall?
And where's his conscience? Let him pay my wall
Before I pay his trees. Sure, if their fruit
Have caught it of his face, they're no great bargain.

Vivius.
A goodly fruit, 'tis like a goodly deed,
That hath so sound a germ, repute of ill
Cannot corrupt it;—deeds, they are the fruits-

Enter Statius.

Statius.
There's news!

Vivius.
And stirring too; your eyes the vouchers.

Statius.
From Rome.

Vivius.
A moment! [Rises and comes forward.

Statius.
Plaudanus killed!

Vivius.
Jove!—is there tumult?

Statius.
Nay, it was the knife,
And not the sword, that slew him.

Vivius.
At whose instance?

Statius.
Scarce known,—or Bassianus, or Severus;
Certain the emperor takes his death in peace.

Vivius.
Ha! carrion-bird, would'st tamper with die eagle?

Statius.
They say the messenger hath brought advices
Touching the Christians.

Vivius.
So — so is it? You see
My warning was not lost. Let me despatch;
There have been " silver crowns " entwin'd with wreaths!

[Returns to his place.

Statius (aside).
What are die chances? If Hilarianus...

Vivius.
Well, of these goodly trees?—this worthy wall?
'Tis pity two brave neighbour-citizens
Should have an ill division standing 'twixt them.
Time wears,—my steward must, with weightier help,
 Make light your difference — for your loss find gain;
For you,—you are content with character?

Second Citizen.
(Aside) And with the trees!—A trifle for my labour.

Vivius.
Well, he shall fit it with you; so depart,
And see that amity remain with you:
Discord is no safe hand to trust with apples.
The next? Why, what a ruddy face is here!
As honest, I'll be sworn; and goodly limbs
To match brave service with as brave a deed.

Enter a Slave (in haste)

What is thy tale?—out with it! Art thou dumb?

Slave.
I saw

Vivius.
Go on! Is't fire?—is't death? What is it?

Slave.
The Lady Vivia

Vivius.
Ha! what of her? Speak!
Slave.

But now the prefect's guards have borne her off.

Vivius.
The prefect's guards!

Slave.
They say she is a Christian.

Third Citizen.
Vivius! — The gods have struck him!

Statius
So—that Jew

Vivius.
The Jew—I see it all!—plain as a scroll;
He and the prefect! Outrage upon her!
O vengeance! this shall fill full to its scope
Thy widest grasp,—gods! Where have they taken her?

Slave.
To prison.

Vivius.
That's relief; anywhere rather
Than to his stew. And yet, 'mong felon slaves,
The loathsome scum of the city,—cag'd in darkness,
Citizens! have you blood within your hearts?
Wives, daughters, in your homes? Rouse all! and know
A governor doth rule within your city
Can drag them forth, and hale them through your streets
All draperied in lies, black as the lust He seeks to appease.

Statius.
Hold! hold! you go too far:
It may be lust for gold; or say revenge.

Vivius.
Or say revenge? Revenge that I have ta'en
The parts of those—your parts, whom he hath left
Neglected, scorn'd, to lead his shameless life
In most unmeasur'd riot, reckless waste

CitizenS.

Shame, shame!—so he has. Shame!

Statius.
(Aside) Go on; that works.

Vivius.
What works? My outrag'd blood is up in arms,
And drums within mine ears; I scarce can hear.

Statius.
(Aside) Tell them he wants the gold that should be theirs.

Vivius.
And for I have some wealth that he doth covet,
He seeks to threat it from me by—(the thought
The very thought doth choke me, ere the word)
Branding the daughter of my house as —Christian!
Seizing her at the altar of her home,
Impiously braving all those deities
Who guard its sacred precincts

Statius.
(Aside) To the gold!
Say, 'ds the people's gold that he would have.

Vivius.
Think—'tis the people's gold that he would clutch;
Then answer, who shall have it, he or you?

Enter Camus and Barac.

Camus.
Nor he nor you; 'ds for the gods to claim

[The citizens fall back. Exit Statius.

The gods she hath defied! They bow in mercy,
Beyond her vain deservings, to accept
The ransom thou canst give for her offence.

Vivius.
Oh, plot most vile! And these are thy accusers,
A ravening priest, a misbegotten Jew,
Back'd by a base-born minion of—of who?
Of what?—a corpse! His power—where is it now?
I do defy him. You! Deal out your wrath
Your wrath—not Jove's! On his Olympian throne,
With brow begirt in majesty of ire,
He's frowning now upon thee, while he grasps
Tight for the hurl th' avenging thunderbolt,
Destin'd for thee, thou desecrating priest!

Away, and with my scorn! Friends, follow me,
Ye who have wives and daughters, for their sake;
And all for Jove's!

Camus.
They fear the power of him,
Whom now, in me, thy impious tongue blasphemes.

Vivius.
Nay, let them fear while breath of thine infects
The city, lest it reach our mighty Dead,
To fan their ashes to a shame so hot,
Shall crack their ums asunder; bid them rush
Up to the heav'ns, in fiery appeal,
For leave to purify their place of rest;
And, earning confirmation of the gods,
Dash down in show'rs of vengeance on us all!
'Tis him that ye should fear! Lo! while I speak,
 Look at him, withering beneath the curse :
Shrunken his form, as yon hot bolt of Jove
Were on the way to smite him into dust.
Beware the doom'd! lest that his doom be yours.
Citizens! follow me; the gods are with us.

[The crowd draw off with Vivius.

Barac.
What will he do?

Camus.
I know he can do nothing.

Barac.
And my reward?

Camus.
Like his,—will come with time.
Now, should the daughter make her recantation,
The father's trapp'd. This stirring of the mob
Hath made him mine. He thinks he knows me!—No,
Not yet to the full. You seek his gold to hoard,
I take his heart to torture.

Barac.
Share alike.

Camus.
Away I

[Exeunt.

SCENE III

House of Statius. Statius and Nola.

Statius.
No more entreaties: that I do deny thee
Sight of her now, thou'lt thank me for hereafter.
I know the world—have paid well for my knowledge;
Thou know'st it not, wouldst hurry towards an ambush,
And when too late, may'st find thyself hemm'd in.

Nola.
Father, quite sure am I, were these same Christians
 As wicked as they say, Vivia had never
Been seen amongst them.

Statius.
That I cannot tell;
I know but little of their lives and doings:
While they reject the worship of our gods,
And trample down the necessary barriers
That guarantee to us just preservation
Of all those wise and nice distinctions, made
For the better ordering of society,
There is enough for me! Were all the good
They may account their own, possess'd by them,
An evil is it to defy old custom,
Outweighing all their good. Your hasty leapers,
Your steppers wide from all the good old ways,
Mar the discreet sobrieties of life;
Be thou well sure that nothing e'er was gain'd
By opposition to establish'd forms.
The wisdom of our fathers found our gods
And laws sufficient—why should we seek others?

Nola.
Dear father, let me go; I know 'tis false:
Vivia is not a Christian!

Statius.
That's no matter:
Enough for me they say that she is one.
Behoves us heedfully to watch our steps
The where they tend, lest we be led 'mongst those
Who have been breath'd upon by ill report,
No matter true or false. In time of plague,
Many are kept apart, and held infect,
Who yet are sound; so must it be with Vivia.
Thus much I know of her,—that she hath stepp'd

Out of the province that befits a woman,
Whose duty is, to keep within the house;
If maiden, subject to her father's will;
If wife, obedient to her husband's rule;
If mother, careful only for her children;
She hath forgot herself,—you must forget her.

Nola.
But you have let Caecilius go!

Statius.
Not so;
He goes against my wish. And thus we see
The evil fruits that even now are showing
Upon this tree, corrupt already, though
Of such latter spring: her disobedience
Unto her parent's will, his unto mine;
Though not my child, he owes obedience still
Unto my guardianship. But this remember,—
For him there's less to fear: I hedge him not
As I would thee. The fortunes of a man
Are of less tender growth than those of woman.
Besides, the harm his foolishness may gender
Would rather fall on her than light on him.
" He is young," "misled," "a victim to her art."
The world will make easy excuse for him;
Not so for thee.

Nola.
I would I were a man!

Statius.
Thou'rt indiscreet, and steppest o'er the bounds
Prescrib'd a maiden's tongue. Go to thy chamber
Stay there; nor have thou speech nor sight of any
Until I lead thee forth in public show
To offer sacrifice unto our gods.

[Exeunt severally.

SCENE IV.

A cell. Vivia alone.

Vivia.
If I could only breathe, or have but one
Of all those myriad idle water-drops
Playing in light around my garden-fountains!
Patience!—I know it, and I would be patient;

Only this whirling round and round within
Strangles those thoughts should bring me strength and peace.
These faces, looking at me through my hands,
These voices, moaning in my ears like winds,
If they would go! Now, now, how loud they are!
All fancy—fancy; reason says 'tis fancy.
The sense is all that's mad. A dreadful story!
So mad 'twill get the better. Air!—To the door.

[She rises.

All things are dizzy; and the slimy wall
Goes sliding down beneath my hands. That flash
Across the eyes,—how real! how like the lightning!
How could the lightning see to find its way?
I know not which is real, and which is mad.
Hark, there's a crash! Sure that was from without.
Silence again. No; a feint cry,— "My child,—"
My child,—he wants me, cries for me. Help! open!
The iron burns; my heart on fire, dries up
The fount should slake the flame consuming him.
Open the door!

Vivius. (without).
My child!—open the door!
Quick!—quick!

Vivia.
My father! Help, Almighty God!

[She sinks.
 Enter Vivius.

Vivius.
Thou call'st on Jupiter! I knew 'twas false.
(Keep open that door,—in mercy, shut it not.)
Vivia, my girl! look up—look up; thou'rt safe!
Thou'rt in thy father's arms. There—courage, courage!
Come, kiss me; wind thine arms about his neck,
Who never knew he lov'd thee until now.
Thou call'st on Jupiter; and he will hear thee!
He, the Great Thunderer, on their heads shall wreak
A tenfold vengeance. Shrink not! us will he spare,
When he beholds how child and father love,
Never till now knew I how well, nor thou.
Thou canst not tell what I will be to thee!
Thou call'st on Jupiter! My hope, my Vivia,
That one appeal unto our ancient god
Summons a thousand deities around
To light thy prison-gloom with radiant promise.
A few short hours, and all our cares are o'er.

Oh! I will lead thee forth, like to a Grace
(As thou wert ever I) deck'd with rosy wreaths,
A chaplet in thy hand, which thou shalt lay
Upon the altar of almighty Jove;
While thousands rend the air with shouts of joy,
To hail alike thy beauty and my triumph!

Vivia.
Oh, speak not thus!

Vivius.
The tone doth startle thee.
How thou dost quiver! Gentle!—I will be gentle
To thee—to those who thus have shatter'd thee

Vivia.
My boy—my Thascius!

Vivius.
Why, what a burst is this?
He shall come to thee. Peace! Nay, nay, thou'rt weak
Lean on me. Cling, cling! I will bear thee yonder.
Gods! and is this thy couch? Stay, let my robe,
There—rest!—Thy father's breast will serve for pillow.

Vivia.
No resting-place for me;—alas, alas!

Vivius.
Rock not thy body thus. What should 1 do?
Jove! what a reck'ning will I have for this!
But listen! There stays one without, who came
Earnest to see thee: 'tis a faithful youth;
For when denied, he laid him down beside
The prison-gate, and ne'er hath stirr'd him since.
See, I will send my tablets by Caecilius,
To bid them bring the child to thee with speed.

Vivia.
Away, my father, thou!

Vivius.
Go for him? well,
Aught for thy peace. And now be well prepar'd:
One trial more—but one ; it is the last.
To-morrow they will lead thee to the Forum.
Fear not; I will be there.

Vivia.
Oh, no, no, no!

Vivius.
What, canst thou doubt it? 'tis thy weakness speaks,
And not thyself. Courage, my Vivia, courage!
The boy shall bring thee ease, and ease bring sleep.
All will go well. I dare not tell thee now
What hopes, what plans:—why, die bare words have thrill'd thee.
I do thee harm; I'll send, not come again:
Though I would be the gentlest nurse, my blood
Leaps to redeem our wrongs. Forgive — farewell!

Vivia.
Forgive! farewell!—oh, those are words for me.
Once more thine arms about me, O my father!

Vivius.
I will not quit thee thus.

Vivia.
You must, you must!
Have I not lov'd thee?

Vivius.
Well.

Vivia.
And love thee still?

Vivius.
Who doubts thy love?

Vivia.
It may be thee, full soon!
But never when home-hours were at their sweetest,
When thou unto thy child didst show the fondest,
And she most loving, gentle to thy will,
Oh, never did she love thee thus, nor pray
As now she prays to heav'n for thee. O God
Our Father, save and bless him!

Vivius.
And bless thee.
Hush, do not speak again—thou art bewilder'd.
Soon, very soon, thy comfort comes; and then
All will be well. These tears again!—no more :
Remember, hope and triumph are the words.
A kiss! Hush!—quiet, quiet! Now, farewell.

SCENE V.

Morning. A court of the prison. Enter Pudens.

Pudens.
That story of the captive and the angel,
Who came to make the night as bright as day,
I heard it long ago, and scarce believ'd it.
Well, I know not; this gracious lady seems
To make the darkness shine: these pris'ners all
Have something in them not like other men.
Such a dream came last night; I have not had
One near so happy since I was a boy.
I'll ne'er believe much harm can be in those
Who help us to good dreams.—Who knocks?

Voice. (without).
The deacons.

Enter Tertius and Pomponius.

Tertius.
How fare the brethren?

Pudens.
All of them the better
For better quarters.

Pomponius.
And Perpetua?

Pudens.
Oh, she is brave since she has seen her child,
And says our prison is a palace for her.

Pomponius
The father—where is he?

Pudens.
Was here last night.

Tertius.
Ay, and what happen'd?

Pomponius.
Said he aught to thee?

Pudens.
Oh, he's a proud one—he but bade me keep
 The door awide, to give the lady air.

Pomponius.
He frighten'd her?

Tertius.
And does she keep the faith?

Pudens.
Nay, I know not: she wept and wept the while,
Till I did nothing hear only her sobs,
And nothing see for tears that came to help her.
She's quiet now as any lamb; —I would
They'd let her bide so.

Tertius.
Shall we pass within?

Pudens.
I'll take you to them all. To look at her,
So white, so young, and yet so mother-like
She gazes on her boy,—'tis a sweet sight!
Scarce seen, ere done: within an hour 'tis like
They're in the Forum.

Tertius.
Christ be with them there!

[Exeunt.

SCENE VI.
Street leading to the Forum.
Citizens passing; others enter.

Second Citizen.
Stay you—a word : what think you of this business?

Fourth Citizen.
Think? I don't stay to think: with Vivius' coin,
A pouch of it, all safe here in my tunic.

First Citizen.
He's but a fool who thinks to buy the people,
Unless he knows the trick to stunt our growth:
A growing good must feed a growing man.
You with your coin — if in this mutiny,
A Roman sword should chance to find it out.
What comes of you, and your coin after you
Both spent. A soldier's not particular;
He'll spill your blood, all in the way of business.

Fourth Citizen.
Mutiny? where's the mutiny?—to shout,

And bear a woman home in triumph? Well,
If that's your mutiny

Second Citizen.
What! are your eyes
Not strong enough to run the length o' your nose
This triumph, as he calls it, is one step,
The first, in his rebellion.

Fourth Citizen.
Where's the harm?
For when he takes the second, we can leave him.

Third Citizen.
Not I—I'll see the end on't on his side;
He's stood by me, and I will stand by him.
'Tis not for want of pains, if he should fail:
He has been late die night, early the morning,
Stirring amongst the people.

Fourth Citizen.
See who come,
The servants of the governor: let's on.

First Citizen.
The drones that waste our honey—idle thieves!

[Exeunt Citizens.
Enter Varro and Servants.

First Servant.
There go more scowlers: such an eye, ye gods!
You say our master's safe—he need be wary.

Varro.
Oh, trust the priest, he knows what he's about;
He's always in the marrow of die matter.

Second Servant.
The money too!—But if we lose the show?

Varro.
No fear—they are all staunch. The lady writ
Her faith this very morn unto her father:
Her messenger was stopp'd— die priest knows why.

Third Servant.
How many are there?

Varro.
Three men and one woman;

Black morsels, two of them. I wonder how
The lady likes her company.

Second Servant.
Bah! for me.

Varro.
One Saturus escap'd—the worst, they say,
For he it was who tempted all the rest.

First Servant.
To what a feed! What beasts are in the city?

Varro.
Oh, none of any count; wild cows, bears, leopards,
None royal.

Second Servant.
Sure a man might match a leopard:
We shall see rare sport belike.

[A shout.

Varro.
Quick, forward!

[Exeunt

SCENE VII.

The Forum

Hilarianus seated: behind him stand Servilius, Lentulus, Naso, Statius, and others. In the centre, Vivia Perpetua, Felicitas, Saturninus, Secundulus and Revocatus.

On the right a statue of SEVERUS. An altar at its foot, at which stands Camus, Barac near him. Tribunes, Lictors, Dolsiers, Citizens; some with clubs, staves.

Lictor.
Silence for the praefect!

Hilarianus.
Here in the name
Of the emperor we sit, his pow'r to us
Entrusted, for the law's full vindication.
For ye who have offended yet remains
Free pardon, so ye offer sacrifice
To yonder image : but withholding this,
Note well the penalty,—a dreadful death

On the morrow in the amphitheatre.
Ye citizens, bear witness all, that mercy
Runs evenly with justice. These prov'd guilty,

[A murmur.

Shall yet have pardon, and be suffer'd free,
So they perform the needful sacrifice.

Servilius.
Excellent, excellent!

Hilarianus.
Pray speak not thou;
'Tis earnest now—no jest; I like it not.
I wait your answer.

Saturninus.
Whose?

Hilarianus.
Yours, and those near you.

Saturninus.
For me, I do defy your emperor.
Sacrifice unto him! Yon marble arm
See, stretching forth, as though he would command it
What doth it stand for?—flesh and blood like this.
 To Jove a like defiance! On his altar,
And on that sensual priest, his minister,
I turn my back in scorn.

Revocatus.
So I. Hearken, ye people

Camus.
Silence, slave!
We like not these long speeches.

Hilarianus.
Answer, you
Who were his fellow-slave.

Felicitas.
Ay, it is true;
I was a slave: now I am one no more.
Ask Saturnin—he will expound for me.
The flesh and blood like mine is not my master!

Hilarianus.
And thou?

Second Servant.
It looks half dead with him already;
He'll not be worth the sport.

Secundulus.
Accept me, Christ; I offer unto thee my soul, my strength:
Would it were more, to do thee worthier service!

Hilarianus.
And these are all?

Saturus (coming forward).
One more.

A Citizen.
That is the man!

Hilarianus.
Hast heard die penalty? Let none here say
We are not just to all.

Saturus.
Long since I knew it.
The penalty was on me when I render'd
The sacrifice that now ye ask. The death
Ye count as such, for us is life eternal.

Hilarianus.
Thou wilt not sacrifice to the emperor's health?

Saturus.
I will invoke the one Almighty Power
To grant him health, and that alone success
A monarch may rejoice in : grant him, God,
A faithful senate and an upright people;
Crown all his acts with love; and be his reign
One universal peace throughout the land!
And so for thee; and these, who are with both
 Equal in right of brotherhood as men,
Peace and good-will!—and (oh, best gift!) to know
The love of Him—of Christ,—who liv'd and died
To sanctify all earth by their possession.
Upon that earth, made by his blest abode
A holy altar evermore to God,
I stand; and for oblation here I offer
The incense of a loving, praising soul
To Christ our Lord,—to God our heavenly Father!

Hilarianus.
Let us depart.

Camus.
Not yet; remains there one.

Second Citizen.
See, see, he is afraid of her—'tis true!
Vivius is in the right. What should we do?

Third Citizen.
Why comes he not?

Hilarianus.
Vivia Perpetua!

Lentulus (aside to Naso).
She's very beautiful.

Naso.
So Camus thinks.

Lentulus.
Somewhat too slight.

Naso.
No hope for either of you.
Whoe'er saw calmness like to that give way?

Hilarianus.
Vivia Perpetua!

First Citizen.
Look, look, there's her father!
There, by that pillar—he was hid behind it.

Hilarianus.
Lady, although suspect (and therefore justice
Must have account of thee), yet be assur'd,
Proving thine innocence, thou wilt appear
More fair, more virtuous.

Vivius.
(Aside) Basest hypocrite!

Hilarianus.
How little asks it of thee! —what the effort?
One wave of that white hand towards yon flame
Shall sign thee faithful to our gods and laws.
Fear not; all are your friends. I wait your answer.

Vivia.
I am a Christian. [Tumult. The crowd shrinks bad.

Vivius. (coming forward).
How! who spoke those words?
Not she—'twas not her voice; believe it not.
Citizens, up! A trick—there is a trick!
Ye have heard of marbles made oracular;
Of stones that had a voice; of trees that utter'd:
Ye know not if yon priest's deceptious art
Look where she stands, bound up as in a spell,
Pale, motionless, unconscious as a statue!
Let her step forth from off that treacherous platform,
And, standing face to face, repeat those words.
You will not hear them—no, she will not say diem!

Vivia (advances a few steps)
I am a Christian.

Vivius.
Still there is some juggle.
Four words—four words in parrot repetition,
What are they? what to prove? What is—a Christian?

Vivia.
Truth above all,—it is the Christian's word;
Love over all,—it is the Christian's soul;
Life beyond all,—it is the Christian's hope:
To lay down mortal life for Christ who liv'd
For Truth and Love, and died for Life Immortal,
 This is to be a Christian.—I am ready.

Vivius.
Is't dream? madness?—who am I ? where am I ?
I wring this hand,—'tis mine, I feel it mine;
I   tear this hair,— still do I feel it mine :
No dream, no madness. Oh, for a sword, to cut,
To pierce me to the heart!—to feel as truly
It is my blood that's pouring on these stones.
Out, out with it! I will not have within
The fount that gave the life to —oh, my child
Thou art my child—behold me at thy feet,
Those feet to tread the necks of emperors,
And why not mine? Unsay, if thou didst say,
Those terrible words; have pity cm thy father!

Hilarianus.
Poor man, I pity thee.

Vivius. (starting up).
Pity!—pity from thee!
Hear, mighty gods! send down your lightning—quick!
Scorch up his pity—wither him who gave it!

Oh, that we dwelt beside that mount of hell,
Whence leapt destruction on the buried city,
That now it might shower forth its fiercest fires,
Making all Carthage one huge heap of ashes,
A hecatomb unto this mighty woe!

Hilarianus.
They strangely move a man, grief and grey hairs
And yet they touch not thee, who art his child!

Vivius.
Reproach unto my age? See there—behold!
I throw it back on thee,—with curses on thee.
Speak not again to her—I do forbid thee.
I, Vivius, her father, who to thee
Do owe no fealty save in loyal hate;
I that am king o'er her, demand my own,
And thus I claim it!
 [He attempts to seize Vivia, and is stricken by a lictor. He falls.

Vivia.
Help — Felicitas!

Camus.
Bear him away—his reck'ning comes hereafter.

Hilarianus.
Let him go free, if he return to life.
The gods be prais'd, 'tis over! Let us go.

Camus.
The sentence!—you have forgot the sentence.

Hilarianus.
True.
To-morrow, being the festival of Geta,
We shall repair to the amphitheatre,
Where you, who are so stout in your resistance,
Must meet the punishment unto your crime. [A shout.

Camus.
Citizens, quietly unto your homes.

ACT THE FIFTH.

SCENE I.

An outer court of the prison.
Enter Pudens.

Pudens.
'Tis hard our Christians may not hold in peace
This their last supper, but upon them comes
The city out, to stare.

[A knocking.

Voices (without).
Open! we're late.

Pudens.
The noise won't make you earlier.

Enter Citizens.

Be quiet!

Fourth Citizen.
Quiet! what's that?—we are come, all of us,
To enjoy ourselves.

Enter Soldiers from within.

A Soldier.
Not much of that, I reckon:
'Tis dull enough. Better along with us
To the gladiators—they are the boys.

[Soldiers pass out.

Citizens.
Come on!
[They enter.
Enter Lentulus, a Slave following.

Lentulus.
O breath! the miserable mob are here;
The air is poison'd. Hither bring that robe:
This place is no curator for the vestments.
Which way?—on with the lamp.

Enter Naso,

Naso.
You here!
Have you no fear of prison-damps and dews
For curls ambrosial?—Nay, let us be grave.
You come to look on beauty; I on strength.
Is the lady with the rest?

Pudens.
But now she was
 Apart, and with her brother.

Naso.
And the father?

Lentulus.
Did he not die under the blow in the Forum?

Pudens.
Nay, sir, he home return'd. 'Tis said he takes
To his daughter's child; lives with it in his arms;
Gives it its food; rocks it like any nurse,
They scarce know if in savageness or love.
He sits with lips hard set, with brows knit close:
The child doth cry, afeard to face his eyes.
His only words have been, a fierce denial
To spare it to the mother for once more!

Naso.
And how takes this the lady—does she weep?

Pudens.
Her eyes are like to eyes that never more
Will know a tear.

Naso.
Come, Lentulus.—What hour
Tomorrow?

[To Pudens.

Lentulus.
For the amphitheatre?

Naso.
Surely,—to see how she who has begun
Her work so bravely, ends it.

Lentulus.
So not I:
To look on beauty, well—but not on blood;
The hands, the garments, ne'er feel pleasant after.

Pudens.
Sirs, would you do kind service? Should you find
The citizens, and those have pass'd within,
Break up with noise or jest the Christians' peace,
You're of some standing, and might keep them down.

Naso.
Good fellow, yes.—Now, Lentulus, draw up!
Your inches and your lordly reputation
Must do their best: command a gaping quiet,
After, perchance, to have your back a target
For blunted arrows from their wagging tongues :
For why?—you mount the wreath, they but the cap;
 Unless you have preferment for the rogues,
And then,— how many Jupiters have we?

Lentulus.
Let me consider.

Naso.
Let us pass within. [All enter.

SCENE II.

A vaulted quadrangle within the prison. A table spread.

Saturus, Saturninus, Vivia Perpetua, Felicitas, Revocatus, and other Christians, seated; Tertius and Pomponius ministering. Attilius and CAecilius standing near Vivia. Citizens, Soldiers, Beg-gars, looking on

Saturninus.
Silence!

A Citizen
For you?—ha, ha!

A Soldier.
I say, old comrade, You'd better have kept to the trade.

Enter Lentulus, Naso, and Pudens. naso.

Silence!

A Citizen.
Who comes?

A Lictor.
Keep the peace here!

Lentulus.
Jove! Naso, look—she's seated next a slave!

Naso.
What wonder next?—there's something in this faith.

Saturus.
And you we now are leaving, let your eyes
 Look on us as on those about to take
Swiftly a journey to that happier land,
Where, midst the joys awaiting us, ofttime
 Our spirits yet will yearn for fuller bliss
To welcome ye, who yet uncall'd remain,
After your toilsome pilgrimage is o'er.
Hold consecrate within your memories
This our last supper, and His ordinance,
Whom we so oft together have remember'd,
When his command to "do this" was unfelt
 For love that leapt to his feet in reverence.
Hold consecrate those praying, watching hours,
In ray-lit darkness held, or full-day'd twilight;
Whether beneath the cypresses, where oft
We talk'd of death leading to endless life;
Or in our cavern dim beside the sea,
Out of the depths we lifted up to Him
Our hearts in song;—to feel this answer come
Down like a sunbeam, cleaving through the dark,
There is nor height nor depth, in heaven or hell,
The radiance of Christ's mercy may not reach!

A Voice.
Who was it that beneath those cypresses
 Did prophesy this end unto ye all?

Saturus.
Who was it that beneath those cypresses
Answer'd, It would come welcom'd, whensoe'er?
He who doth now beneath a deeper gloom
The searchless shadow of death's silent wings
Pray that thine hour, whene'er it come, may find
A heart as calm, and from a trust as sure.

A Voice.
I want no pray'r of thine; best pray for those
Who tremble round thee at their coming doom.

Saturus.
Answer me, fellow-martyrs! Is there one
Would now resign his privilege to die?

Vivia.
And if there be, let him forbear a while :
Ere he yield up his passport into heaven,
I would make known a vision from the Lord,
His gracious answer to a pray'r for sign
Might satisfy my brother of the end.
I saw a ladder reaching to the skies :

Near to its foot a scaly dragon crouch'd;
And by its upward sides all instruments
That ruthless, wretched men employ for torture
(More pitiable they than those they scathe).
This ladder, like a voice I needs must follow,
Drew me towards it; but ere I was there,
Saturus was before me, and I saw him,
Quick, like an angel's flight, ascend on high.
I saw his face as now; he turn'd it full
And pityingly upon me, and his words
Are fresh as those he spoke but now unto us.
1 hear them still: " Perpetua, 1 await you!
Beware the dragon, that he do not tear you!"
Then I invok'd the name of Christ, believing:
And all in faith, and no part in me fear,
I stepp'd upon the ladder—so on the dragon.
Stepp'd?—say, 'twas flight!—no time to think of pain,
For heaven's joy came down like heaven's light
To meet me on the way. Erel was there,
A dawn more clear than earthly skies e'er saw
Was all around me, brightening as I rose:
Sweet airs from angels' wings fann'd soothingly,
Wafting their sweeter voices;—so I came
To the realm of rest, soaring in light and song!
O garden of the Lord! O Paradise!
O streams that murmur'd music as they flow!
As living fountains newly loos'd in spring
Sing shining to the sun that gave them freedom,
These sung of love, where God is all in all
O lofty presence, though in shepherd-guise,
Of him who led his flocks beside those waters ;
While blessed souls, in raiment white as snow,
A multitude, their feet as noiseless falling,
Still follow'd on the steps of their Redeemer,
And, oh, the voice that welcom'd me his daughter!
(Attilius, tell my father of this vision;
And say I did remember him in heaven!)
He gave me then a draught of new-drawn milk;
But scarce receiv'd this sacrament of heaven,
When all the voices of those blessed ones
Rang out in songs of joy. The sound s well'd forth
Up to the highest heaven; till echoes came,
Sent from the angels round the throne of God.
Hallelujah! amen! and I awoke,
The heavenly strain yet ringing in the air!
Still doth it linger, to bear up on high
Our faithful voices Lift them to the Lord!

Voices of all the Christians.
"Hallelujah! amen! for the Lord God Omnipotent reigneth."

Attilius.
Thy voice is sacrificial flame, my sister;
Thine eyes they burn like stars.

Vivia.
Heaven hath descended!

Naso.
May a stranger speak with you,—one who would ask
In earnestness as earnestness deserves?

Vivia.
Whate'er thou wilt.

Naso.
I would some questions solve
That beat about for answer, while I look
At you and at your fate.

Vivia.
Speak on.

Naso.
Your God,—
You say he is all love; yet he condemns you
To such a death?

Vivia.
Say to such life eternal!
And were there only death,—no life beyond,
He hath so miracled my soul with gifts
In these last hours, that I for such a God
Would die; nor scarcely feel in death a pang,
For joy and wonder at his mighty power.

Naso.
Your spirit soars in triumph! Yet 'tis won
By sacrifice of all your human love?
All the affections once so dearly prised
Cast off —forgotten!

Vivia.
(Christ, thou knowest0—Not so.
They are beneath the wings, and 1 will bear them
Up to His throne, and He, in that great love
You do deny him,—oh! he will receive diem;
And Christ, for whom I die, will plead for them
I know he will; and thus comes death to me,
To free me, that I see him face to face,
To implore his grace for those I lov'd on earth.

Naso.
I could—almost I could, bid thee implore
A grace for me! Yet answer me once more,
You die for Christ, you say; he cannot need
The death of one like thee?

Vivia.
I need to die.
I could not live,—could'st thou?—to feel a truth
Cry loudly in the heart, and strangle it.
Were this the end, no other life beyond,
Better to perish thus, our dust unurn'd
(So it might nourish still a living flower),
Rather than breathe such breath as hourly kills
The truth that blooms within.
Naso.

This truth in thee?

Vivia,
I do believe all men have equal claim;
Or mightiest emperor, or meanest slave:
For one great God, he did create us all!
To him; and unto Christ,—as unto him
Who liv'd and died to atone us with the Father,
My worship rises. Should I sacrifice
To the emperor,—to Jove, believing this?

Naso.
For criminals!—claim or regard for them?

Vivia.
In pity: that doth sadden o'er their error;
For, seeming good howe'er to them, 'tis yet
Consummate loss. Oh, blessed Christ, who ne'er
Could bid us hate a sin ere he would say,
"Compassionate the sinner." With what gifts
He sought to win them,—hope, love, life immortal!

Naso.
Thou dost believe that all unto this heaven
Of love will come at last?

Vivia.
Christ said, "with God All things are possible!" and God is love.

Naso.
But what were left to us, the work achiev'd?
Each having gain'd an entrance to this heaven,
There were no more to do.

Vivia.
Oh, have you not
A life within, that asks another life
For its unfolding? Hast not felt thy soul
To swell and press against this limiting earth?
Hast never thirsted for a perfect truth?
Hast never long'd to meet with what should
fill Full to its large desire thy sense of praise?
To praise—praise infinitely, were enough.
To dwell for ever with the Great Perfection,
The one untiring, ever-moving spirit
Of Good,—what were it! Then to have reveal'd
By light, the element wherein he dwells,
His mighty plans, wrought out of one great law,
The law of love. No longer mystery:
Faith turn'd to sight, as promis'd of the Lord.
Think with what joy, what loving adoration,
Would burst the song of praise from forth our souls,
Praise that had gain'd increas'd intelligence,
To meet the work of His intelligence,
When with our upturn'd eyes, we reach'd the height,
Where, like the beams of his own sun on the mountain,
Rested the all-seeing gaze of the Creator
Over the world he made; and he proclaim'd That "All was good! "

Naso.
Beautiful prophetess,
Thou shalt not die!

Vivia.
He reads;—hush! let us listen.

Saturus (reading from a scroll).
"Except a corn of wheat fall into the ground and die, it abideth alone; but if it die, it bringeth forth much fruit".

Lentulus.
Where is that pallid quiet man was with thee
In the Forum?

Tertius.
Paler and quieter now!
We scarce had enter'd in the prison-gates
Ere he sank down. A smile was on his face;
He wears it yet—in death!—as I shall do
Long in my mem'ry, as an old man may.
Ah, sir! as there he lies, like smiling marble
A monument of Christian grace—there comes
A voice from forth the quiet of that smile:
He being dead, yet speaketh of the peace
Those only know in death who know the Lord.

Lentulus.
Naso, this place is like an ague to me,
Hot, stifling, pent, and yet my blood is ice.
I am going: you will sup with me to-morrow,
And tell me of these doings of the morning?

Naso.
I shall not go to the amphitheatre.

Lentulus.
Not go?

Naso.
Good night.

[Exit Naso,

Lentulus.
Stay, stay; leave me not here!

[Exit Lentulus.

First Citizen.
Where are they off to? let us follow them.

Second Citizen.
And is this all they do? 'tis hard, methink,
To have them up for this.

Soldier.
Oh, they are cunning.
I have heard people say, and great ones too,
They always eat a child before they've done.
When is that coming on?

Tertius.
Come, all ye poor:
We have not much to give; and yet these fragments,
And such as these, have had the blessing rich
Of Him who came to feed the poor like ye,
E'en with the bread of life. Depart in peace!

Beggars.
Great Jove reward ye all!

[Exeunt.

Barac (comes forward).
You see me now.

First Soldier.
Ha! pay me the coin I won of you.

[Exit Barac

Holloa there!

[Exeunt Soldiers and Citizens.

Vivia.
My brother, we must part. Hast thou no word
Not one—of hope that we shall meet again?

Attilius.
Would I were Christian too, to die with thee!

Vivia.
Live to be one, and live eternally!
Thou wilt, I do believe it, my Attilius.
Give me thy hand, and let it be for token
That thou believ'st it too. Oh, clasp it, clasp it!
I do believe this very death I die
Do not relax thy grasp—shall lead the way
 For those I love to heaven!

Saturus.
Part in peace!

Voices OF THE Christians.
Part in peace! Christ's life was peace,
Let us live our life in him!
Part in peace! Christ's death was peace,
Let us die our death in him!
Part in peace! Christ promise gave
 Of a life beyond the grave,
Where all mortal partings cease.
Part in peace!

Attilius.
Is there such life?

Vivia.
My brother, part in peace.

[Exit Attilius. The Christians separate.

Caecilius, go not thou.—Gaoler, give leave.
Nay, quench the lights,—my lamp will serve; and ere
The prison-rounds are o'er, this youth shall meet thee
At the outer gate.

Pudens
Thy time, how long soe'er

[Exit.

Vivia.
I have not spoke with thee tonight, Caecilius :
The slightest word had made the ready tears
Brim o'er their boundaries. Said I not?—weep on!
Thou hast wept to me before, and I with thee.
Ease thy full heart; then be thou strong to listen.
I need thee ;—thou canst help me, if thou wilt.

Caecilius.
Help thee?—and if I will!

Vivia.
But ere I speak
Of the one only thought 'twixt me and heaven,
Tell me of Nola; for my heart is yearning
To see her once again before I die.

Caecilius.
She stays within her chamber; was forbid
To haste to you. She stays in sure belief
That you will be releas'd, will come to her.

Vivia.
Releas'd I shall be! She must come to me.

[She takes a golden arrow from her hair.

Give her this token. Say, our early love
Is fresh with me, as though 'twere yesterday
We wander'd, arm-encircl'd, gathering shells.
Could it be yesterday she talk'd of it?—
Tell her, that He for whom I die was one
Who taught all love to hope: so bid her thought
Soar up, to meet my blessing on the way.
Sure, unforgotten as she is in death,
I still may be her friend in heav'n!—Your thoughts?
They wander.

Caecilius.
They are still with thee!—with thee,
And with the morrow.

Vivia.
Mark me! many thoughts
In many morrows I now ask of thee.
Much has been said—too much—of loving kindness

Render'd to one who was left motherless;
This time to-morrow—Thascius—wilt thou

Caecilius.
Will I? oh, find thy words to tell me what!

Vivia.
Thou'rt young; hast many years—and be they blest
Before thee. I have mark'd a strength in thee,
Seen most within these latter days of trial;
And Heav'n hath prosper'd so the thought that thou
Wilt come to hold the faith; I unto thee,
Commit in trust this child, my Thascius,
In trust unto thy thought. It may be years
Never, perchance—ere act of thine may serve ;
Still let him have a home within thy thought.
And thy good strength, and youth, and years to come,
And fate alike, so oft a loving bond,
And something for his mother's memory,
No, no, there needs no word of thine, Caecilius;
That look has laid an answer at my heart!
Blessing of Heav'n descend on thee and him!

Caecilius.
I would I were your God, to give you wings
Now, now to bear you up! I would not stay you,
Though they would take you quite away from me.
But, oh, that morrow's doom!

Vivia.
Why fear it thus?
The pain of martyrdom dwells not in death.
Think'st thou the love that dares it hath not joy
In loving, to make light the keenest pangs
That touch the body? No!—the torture comes,
And sharpen'd fangs are busiest at the heart,
When all the old affections are dragg'd forth,
And torn upon the rack. What is't to die?

Caecilius.
To sink in quiet 'neath a sighing tree,
Like to the warrior in the song you lov'd;
To die like him, lapsing in quiet shadow,
Were peace : but, oh, the death that waits for thee!—The glare—the tumult!

Vivia.
What are they? since I
Have sat alone, girt with the dreadful dark,
The never-ceasing night, with that one image
In terrible light, stern, pale, and palpable,
The image of my father in his grief:

Eyes shut—the same—or staring wide again,
Still would it come—look, look, now while I speak!

[Vivius appears with a lamp at the opposite side of the quadrangle. He comes slowly forward. The father and daughter gaze at each other for some time without speaking,

Vivius
Do ye know me, who I am?—no, no—no wonder!
I am older many years since yester morn.
I was before that time a man nam'd Vivius,
A happy father, who did read his hopes
Upon the noble brows, and, as he thought,
The most true brows, of a beloved daughter!
I am—I know not what. And when I ask
Help of the outward universe to bring
 Back to myself the former consciousness,
The sun shuts up the while I look on him;
The stars all hurry past me while I pray;
The earth sinks from my feet: all false! all false!

Vivia.
No bitterness now!

Vivius.
No bitterness?—gods,
No bitterness! [He weeps.

Vivia.
My father, that thou couldst
Crowd all thyself at once into one thought!
Think of the faith—look on me as I stand,
A creature anguished at thy agony,
How far beyond the morrow's suffering!
One who hath lost even the few brief hours
She reckoned as her own, to tend her child;
Then think upon the faith that bids my heart
Have yet beneath it all, a hope as calm
As were his lids, when last I parted from him.
Whence comes such miracle—of whom such faith?

Vivius.
Faith! faith! —is that the word?—and miracle!
Yes!—that thy tongue would stir to speak the word!
What is thy faith?—a lie. What are its fruits?
What made thee false to me? What made thee thus
Show forth fine joys to woo me in thy face,
A black'ning plague-spot hidden in thy breast;
Lur'd me to build my trust on thee for rock,
While thou wert rotten as the poisonous heap
The sea throws up for waste? And this is faith!
A lie!—it is a lie!

Vivia.

No more! forbear!
I see, though thou dost not, God's angel stand
Shelt'ring my hope in thee! Thou shalt not speak,
Lest he be moved to stretch a ruffled wing
Up to the Lord, with those accusing words.
I will not have thee less before the Lord
When I shall plead for thee—as plead I will
Plead for the earthly father, who once taught
His child in youth to love the truth, so led
Unto the heav'nly. Hath it been gainsay'd?
Thou know'st it hath not. Thou dost know 'twas love,
 And love alone, that, fearful of thy grief,
Delay'd to bring it on thee, hoping still
A way might show to mitigate the pang.
And I will not be lesser than I am,
Unworthy as I am for this emprise;
For thy sake, not. 'Twas thou who mad'st me true,
And true I am; 'twas thou who mad'st me dare,
And I have dar'd. Who was it in my youth
Did crown our Dido empress of my soul,
For that she gave her blood for double worth,
A faith unbroken, and her people's good?
Did tell me of the wife of Asdrubal,
How that she lov'd the honour of her Carthage
More than her life, and leapt from off the walls
Giving herself, her children, to the flames?
My Carthage is the world! I do but stretch
The line they held—Christ guiding still my hand,
Who first did point the way.

Vivius.

And can it be
Thou art that very child so oft hath stood
 Between my knees to listen those old tales?
Oh for that child again!

Vivia.

I am that child
In all that's simple truth. It was your wont
To question, that an answering lisp might come
Of names, of things, almost too large for one
Of infant speech. Ask me of this,—what is it?
Why, I should say, it is a water-cruise;
I know it that, and could not say it other.
I   could no more deny to those who ask
Of me, what am I;—I do know myself
A Christian, and must say I am a Christian.

Vivius.

Thy breath comes to me like the sharpen'd air
To cut my heart in twain; cold,—cold. But, no!
Here's fire enough. And I will show the world
White ashes yet may cover glowing heat!
You had a boy.

Vivia.
Dead?

Vivius.
To you!

Vivia.
Oh, cruel!—
Oh, spare me, for 'tis here that I am weak.
No, no, spare not; 'tis here I would be strong,
And, trust Christ's mercy, he will guard a child
Blest by such love as mine hath had upon him.
Such love, sure am I, it can never perish.
E'en now doth comfort, like a flower, spring up
Sudden within my breast. You—you,—I know
That you will nourish him—will cherish him,
Will teach his tongue the truth you taught to mine;
 (And hath not Christ abundant for the rest?)
And when that he and time have smil'd down sorrow,
Oft will you, while you sit and gaze on him,
See his dead mother live from out his eyes,
His loving eyes; and then,— dear child I dear father!

Vivius. (falling at her feet).
You weep I—you weep! Oh let those tears at once
Revive my dying hopes like dew, and quench T
he fire that's smouldering in a tortur'd brain.
Once more; yet save me—save thyself;—thou canst
'Tis not too late. Although the storm hangs black,
A word can wave it off, and bring us heaven!
Oh save me from a poison'd, livid past!
Oh save me from a future, that doth yawn
A flaming gulf of hell before my feet!
These are thy father's hands that clasp thy knees;
These are his lips, that on thy very feet
Now print their hope for mercy. Save me!—save me

Vivia,
Oh that my blood had double tide, that I
Might die another death for thy salvation!
Up—up, my father!—my own noble father!
It is thyself in me that stands erect;
Claim kindred with thine own.

Vivius.

Thou teachest well.
I thank thee for thy counsel,—this the last
That we shall take together. I am up;
But not to claim. Utterly I disclaim
All kindred with thee! Blood thou'rt none of mine.
Blood thou hast none in thee; thy heart is stone.
Weakness in me to pray, to weep to it;
Weakness in thee, that thou dost blindly scan
The doom that darkly gathers o'er our house.
E'en now the Fates begin with busy finger
To weave the dusky web shall dimly shroud
Him, the devoted of a mother's shame!
Where is the hope that I should cherish him,
Poor sickly sapling, 'neath a blasted tree?
All wreck'd, near mad, 'tis like they may decree
That I, my brain on fire, my senses gone,
Wild with an agony of memory,
Taking him for my grief, should swing him thus,
And dash the life from out him!

Vivia.
Oh for mercy!

Caecilius.
The trust will hold, although no word was said.

Vivius.
Thou here? Come, I must have a vow of thee.
Hearken, young sir! Swear by thy mother's dust
Or hath this faith made it but rottenness?
Good boy! good boy! — truer unto dead bones
Than others unto living quivering flesh.
Yet swear!—that if in after-life you cross
The path of him was yesterday her child
For he must live in double orphanage,
Unbless'd with e'en the memory of a mother
Ne'er to make known to him—to him or any,
That he did hold communion with her blood.

Caecilius.
I will not take such oath!

Vivius.
How! (seizing him)
Let me feel it
Come up thy throat! Speak! or

Vivia.
Caecilius, do it.

Caecilius.

I swear!

Vivius.
'Tis well. And now, farewell to all
To thee, who art the corpse of all my hopes
Unurned, unburied, ever so to be.
O hell! my very words do twist their sense
 Like tortuous snakes, to sting me as I speak.
Curses on Cartilage!—curses on her people!
Would that tomorrow's crowds might find the earth,
Treacherous as they, give way beneath them all,
And, with one gape of its devouring jaws,
Swallow them quick. 'Twill come, or soon or late,
The flame, the sword, and mighty desolation.
The Goth shall trample where your gardens flourish'd,
Scattering your children like the weeds they grew.

Vivia.
O Christ, who wept over Jerusalem!

Vivius.
Weep thou, and for thine own—no longer thine
(Of little heed). Let me but have the pow'r
To fix these loosen'd wits, I'll make of him
One, who would turn thy love into a curse.
Hope quickens with the thought—there's much to do:
Time narrows in, and I stay here! Away!
Thascius shall be a conqueror—shall hew
His path through this thy faith. Thou sacrifice
Hast chosen ; —mark me! sacrifice shall be
His very end of life; his highest triumph
Won by the sword; and Fame, with crimson hands,
Shall steep in blood the wreath that crowns his brow.
Away! away!

[Exit Vivius.

Vivia.
Caecilius, follow him!
My hope lives in thee, as thou wert Christ's angel.
Tomorrow, at the last, bring me thy tidings.

Caecilius.
Tomorrow!

Vivia.
Speak not word (nor look) to mar
My trust in thee.

[Exit Caecilius.]

My trust, O God, in thee!

[She kneels.

So sure, I have no words that come as prayer.
Thou who dost all things well, shall I of thee
Crave other than thou dost? And, blessed Christ,
 'Twas thou who bad'st us visit in their need
The widow and die fatherless, I know
Thou wilt take pity on a childless father.
Thou, the good Shepherd, who didst gently fold
Those little ones, with blessing, in thine arms,
Wilt care for him, my tender one—my yearling,
Else all bereft.—One prayer—but one—die last:
That in the final hours of this frail life,
With love and praise triumphant over all,
We may shew forth thy glory, blessed Lord. [She rises.
Now to my rest. Not yet—a little while. [Exit.

SCENE III.

Morning. The gate of the amphitheatre.
A throng of Citizens, Soldiers, assembled. Barac near the gate.

A Lictor.
Back there—fall back. Gods! how the fellows swarm;
Enough to fill another hive like that
Within

A Soldier.
Ay, ay; they want a thinning.

First Citizen.
He curs'd us all! I told you 'twas himself,
Not us, that Vivius car'd for. Trust my word,
Jove scorns to take such curses; throws them back
To whence they came.

Third Citizen.
Last night when I went home,
My children still my welcome, 'twas to feel
As seldom feels the poor man with the rich ;
We were both men, both fathers,—happier I
Than he; and well I wish'd him like as I.

A Soldier.
Trumpets, hark!

Enter a Lictor.

Lictor.
Make way here, right and left
The praefect comes; and sure in such a mood!
More mad than mood. I ne'er saw man so chang'd.

Enter in procession Hilarianus, Camus, Statius, Servilius, and others; a Tribune; Officers bearing robes; Trumpeters, Guards-.

Hilarianus.
Lictors, is this the way I bade ye clear?
Yield up your rods to nurses, to fright babes;
The air is mobb'd with breaths as the earth with bodies;
The gate looks ruddy, as with heat—or blood!
Camus, I would my office, like to thine,
Forbade my looking on a corpse.

Camus.
Wer't lawful,
I would exchange the hour with thee.

Hilarianus.
Way there!

[Enters the gate with his train. Camus, Tribune, Guards, Officers, remain waiting without.

Camus.
Tribune, it is not well to array our slaves
(Though it be mockery) in the sacred garb
That services the gods.

Tribune.
One is no slave!

Barac.
Oh, triumph, triumph,—for an age of scorn!
Oft hath the wish been hungry at my heart,
That I had help'd to mock him in the purple,
"Hail, king of the Jews!" Food, food, to see
His followers forc'd these heathen robes to wear;
Whose clip will bite more near their cringing souls
Than all those sharpen'd teeth that wait within.

Tribune.
She comes!

Camus.
I see her not.

Tribune.
Her voice in the air!

Barac.
Hail, priests of Saturn!—priestesses of Ceres!
Good! This it is to see a martyrdom.

Enter singing Vivia Perpetua, Felicitas, Saturus, Saturninus, Revocatus. Guards.

Arise,
My soul arise!
Sing with thy latest breath
Christ's conquest over death.
Arise,
My soul arise!
Sing it unto the skies.
Sing it over the earth and under;
There, 'mongst the myriad graves
Of kings or slaves,
Let the song pierce their urns asunder.

Arise,
Our souls arise!
In heaven the angel-band
Stand ready, in each hand
A palm to wave.
On earth a listening throng
 Wait the redeeming song
Their souls to save.
Below, all silently,
The dead attend the cry,
O grave,
Where is thy victory?
The branches wave,
Our Lord hath risen on high!
O death,
Where is thy sting?
The dust beneath Stirs while we sing,
O grave, where is thy victory?
O   death, where is thy sting?
Arise,
Our souls arise!

Lictor.
Halt at the gate!

Tribune.
This robing ceremony,
Custom, not I, enforces it upon you.

Saturninus.
And I to custom will my body's force
Oppose. Your guards shall hack me limb from limb

Ere I will die swath'd in idolatrous robes,
Leaving my corpse a badge unto the heathen!

Tribune.
Guards, do your office!

Barac.
Hail, high-priest of Saturn!

Saturus.
Tribune, thou'rt held to be a man most just.
Should we, who give the treasure of our lives
As purchase for our right to worship Christ,
Have this dishonour put upon us? Say,
Is't justice in your wars to take a ransom,
Holding the while the captive it should free?
In peace, is't honour to evade a bond,
More sacred for a trust, no record held?
We claim'd exemption from all heathen rites:
The price was death—we come to pay that price.
Wouldst make thyself a debtor in our deaths,
Take from us all, nor give the fair return?

Tribune.
Custom must rule in this. Guards, do your office!

Vivia.
Claudius, a grace!—the last I ask of thee.
Put not this seeming on us; let us show
For what we are. Thou hast an only daughter:
Say, were she dead—Heav'n give her happy life!
If one should seek to dress her senseless corpse
In habit of a slave? No, no, you will not,
I see you will not. We have living souls;
These are to us the habits of a slave.
Spare us in this; and when thy child thou seest,
Say, thou returnest home a man enrich'd;
The blessing of the dying be upon thee!

Tribune.
Pass all within!

[The martyrs pass under the arch singing:

O grave, where is thy victory?
O Death, where is thy sting?
Arise!
Our souls arise!

Tribune.
She flies to death like Fame that wings a triumph!

Soldier.
Well, I could pity her, but back it glances
Like an arrow from a shield.

First Citizen.
'Tis such a sight
As makes a man think twice. Ay, had her father
But lov'd the people well as she her God!
Let us away.

Camus.
Fame, said'st thou? and triumph?
The death she seeks brings infamy on all
Who share her obstinate blood. The Furies now
Lay their keen vipers to her father's heart;
And from henceforth her child I do devote
To whatsoever shame may show most vile,
Just retribution that the gods decree!

Barac.
'Twere time for harvesting.

Camus.
What moves the people?

Tribune.
Look! look!—yon smoke—there, by his sycamores
The oldest in the city—well I know them.
Furies, said'st thou? Vivius hath stol'n their torch;
His house, perchance himself, will soon be ashes!

[Exit Barac.

Camus.
Vengeance, yet hold! [Exit.

Tribune.
Lictors, go seek a guard.
Bring them! — see where bursts forth yon flame!

Mob.
A fire! a fire!   [Exeunt.

SCENE IV.

The Gate Sanevivaria.
Tertius, Pomponius, Testus, and other Christians. Caecilius apart, leaning against the gate.

Tertius.
The clouds are heavy as the day. More like
A gloomy eve, when winter's drawing on,
Than morning towards the spring.

Pomponius.
The heavens are sad
Even at the deeds they do permit. Thus came
The darkness mourning o'er the day that saw
His death on Calvary.

Caecilius.
What means that shout?

Tertius.
That now a Christian's soul ascends to God.

Enter Pudens from the gate.

Pudens.
He gave me this who even now hath died
Under the leopard's fangs.

Pomponius.
Saturus' ring.

Pudens.
But yesterday, he bade me note the words
Here graved upon it,—"Faithful unto death!"
He bath'd it in his blood, then gave it me
With words scarce heard: I could but look at him.
Many have I seen die: upon them all
A shadow fell; on him there shone a light
Most strange. No sunshine was about the place,
But all seem'd darkness there, save only he.

Caecilius.
And yet remains.

[Shouts from within.

Pudens.
I must not stay. Guard well
This precious pledge. A soldier mark'd the gift;
In case of question, safer 'twere with thee.

[Exit Pudens. Shouts from within.

Testus.
O Christ, receive their souls!

Enter Attilius.

Attilius,
The elements
Dissolve. Remains there naught save fire and blood!
Hast seen her?—

Caecilius.
Nay!

Attilius.
The promis'd words—the last,
Woe! woe! that she will ever hear—the home
Where first her eyes were open'd to the light,
But now I saw it fall!

Tertius.
Her father?

Caecilius.
Child?

Pomponius.
Break off!—behold!

Vivia and Felicitas appear; wounded, and staggering under the gateway. A guard on either side.

Attilius.
Gods! what a sight is this!

Tertius.
She seems entranc'd, like one that hath a vision.

Caecilius.
Oh, speak to us once more!

Pomponius.
Whom seekest thou!

Vivia.
Felicitas?—Thou'rt faint! Lean on me—there.

Attilius.
O heavens! the blood is streaming from thy breast

Vivia.
'Tis nothing, nothing, since I knew it not.
And now thy latest tidings.

Attilius.
O my sister,

Thy father's house no longer stands in Carthage!

Vivia.
He, and my Thascius?

Attilius.
Are on the sea.

Caecilius.
Bound whither?

Attilius
That alone do know the heavens
Above the sea.

Vivia.
And God above the heavens!   [Enter a Lictor.

Lictor.
The people clamour, and the swordsman waits,

Felicitas.
Let me stay here—I cannot go within!
My death is all they call for. I am dying.

Vivia.
Courage, Felicitas!—my sister, peace!   [Kisses her.
A few short moments, and we are with Christ.
Farewell I—it is no word—and yet, farewell!
My blessing—oh, my blessing—take once more,
My brothers, brethren all! And if, Caecilius,
Thou and my Thascius meet, tell him, although
No mother's name he knows, a mother's love
Clung round him with her life; a mother's heart
Yearn'd for him in her death; a mother's pray'r
Was her last utterance. My child! my Thascius!
Christ, make him thine!— though baptism such as this
May be the way thy wisdom seest best
To bring him to his mother's arms in heaven!

Vivia throws her arm round Felicitas, and they pass within the gate.

A silence.

Tertius.
There comes no shout—all still as death.

Attilius.
As death!

Prolonged silence.

Enter Pudens.

Pudens.
All's over!—or begun : for if she fell
 On earth, or rose an angel to die skies,
I scarce can tell, for wonder at the sight.
Life seem'd to gather in her as she mov'd
Towards her death; while with her arms—such strength
Most strange in one so delicate—she still
Held up Felicitas; who, sinking fast,
No sooner reach'd the spot where all was ready,
Than down she dropp'd, dead, at Perpetua's feet!
The lady straight unclasp'd her drapery rich,
And laid it o'er the slave as tenderly
As though it were her child. And then she rose
And like a marble pillar there she stood,
As firm, upon the earth. No signal came,
Till she herself did gently bow her head,
And cross her hands upon her breast, in token
Of readiness for the sword. And when the swordsman,
For youth,—or shame to pierce such willingness,
Or awe, more like, of such a presence,—lost
All mastery of his hands to guide his weapon,
Herself did turn the point against her throat,
Her hand plac'd thus, as rest unto his aim :
A word to encourage him—and it was finish'd!

Tertius.
The brethren?— say!

Pudens.
By now, their lives are ended!

Attilius.
From this time forth I do abjure the gods
Who claim such sacrifice.

Tertius.
Turn thou to Christ.

Attilius.
And yet he doth permit

Caecilius.
Oh, do not question!
There came a glory on her face but now
When she invok'd his blessing on her child!
It lingers yet.

Tertius.
See—yonder, who are those

That come upon us?

Pudens.
Camus the priest, and

Attilius.
No priest—no Jove—no gods!

[Exit Attilius.

Tertius.
Let us away!
We meet again for prayer. Though thinn'd the flock,
Still the good Shepherd watcheth, and his crook
Will fold us in. My brethren, go in peace.

[Exeunt all but Caecilius.

Caecilius.
What god should take my vow?—Into the air,
Up to the sun,—unknowing whom to invoke,
Or clouds to bear it to the throne of Jove,
Or angels to the heaven of her Christ,
Here do I dedicate limbs, heart, and life,
Unto the service of her memory!
Sleep, shun the eyes that open on a day
Unspent in watching worship of my trust;
Rest, fail the wandering feet that slack their speed,
 Or weary, though a wayfaring of years
Should stretch before them, ere I see this child
Stand face to face before his mother's soul!
Her name?—will not the very air he breathes
Whisper it to him; and the sky above
Look conscious of her, finding 'mongst the stars
Myriads of voices still to speak of her?
Her name? — there is no other sound. E'en now,
Doth it not fill the universal space,
As though that name had been ere time begun
And evermore would be, though time might end?
Vivia Perpetua!—from the arch it echoes,
Vivia Perpetua!

Enter Camus and Guards.

A Lictor.
Here's one of them!

Camus.
The ward of Statius this. What of the Jew?

A Soldier.

Blacken'd and crush'd beneath a granary-beam
I saw his corpse. Seeking for gold, he met
His fate—deserv'd it. What! the noble Vivius
Make rats his treasurers?

Camus.
Quick!—clear the wreck.
First gather in the goods due to the temple,
Then on a close pursuit. And, soldiers, mark!
A noble price I set upon the child
Of her who now hath died for disobedience.
How?—shall he 'scape me? Rather to the search
Give all the strength of my remaining days!
Nor mountain-fastness, nor remotest cave,
Nor sea how wide soe'er, nor farthest land,
Shall save him from my grasp! Come, thou good youth,
 Away with me!

Caecilius.
I FOLLOW ON THY TRACK.

Thascius (Caecilius) Cyprianus, of unknown parentage, was made a proselyte to the Christian faith by Caecilius a presbyter, whose name he afterwards assumed. He was elected bishop of Carthage A.D. 249, and suffered martyrdom by the sword A.D. 258.

THE END.

www.ingramcontent.com/pod-product-compliance
Lightning Source LLC
Chambersburg PA
CBHW060118050426
42448CB00010B/1932